John D. Voelker
June 29, 1903 - March 18, 1991

TROUT MAGIC

John D. Voelker

TROUT MAGIC

Illustrated by Milton C. Weiler

N

Northmont Publishing Company, Inc.
West Bloomfield, Michigan

ISBN 1–878005–50–2 Cl

Contents

TESTAMENT OF A FISHERMAN

I fish because I love to; because I love the environs where trout are found, which are invariably beautiful, and hate the environs where crowds of people are found, which are invariably ugly; because of all the television commercials, cocktail parties, and assorted social posturing I thus escape; because, in a world where most men seem to spend their lives doing things they hate, my fishing is at once an endless source of delight and an act of small rebellion; because trout do not lie or cheat and cannot be bought or bribed or impressed by power, but respond only to quietude and humility and endless patience; because I suspect that men are going along this way for the last time, and I for one don't want to waste the trip; because mercifully there are no telephones on trout waters; because only in the woods can I find solitude without loneliness; because bourbon out of an old tin cup always tastes better out there; because maybe one day I will catch a mermaid; and, finally, not because I regard fishing as being so terribly important but because I suspect that so many of the other concerns of men are equally unimportant — and not nearly so much fun.

1 Sins My Father Taught Me

(With apologies to him and Dvorak)

1

To paraphrase a deceased patriot, I regret that I have but one life to give to my fly-fishing. I also regret all the years I wasted bait-fishing as well as all the trout I thereby unwittingly maimed or killed by these crude methods. For this is the "sin" my father taught me which I now wish to bewail—the wrong way to fish—though I suppose the way one learns to fish is just as chancy as the color of one's eyes or indeed that one was ever born at all.

In my father's favor I should add that he in turn probably learned his way of fishing from his own father, as I suspect most young fishermen do, and that this tends to happen for a variety of reasons: juvenile hero worship ("My old man's a better fisherman than your old man"); plain simian imitation; a lack of opportunity to learn any other way; and, more practically, the availability of his equipment when the old boy's off at work.

In any case, my youthful corruption began early and soon became total, and by the time I was ten I could wind up and heave a writhing gob of angleworms almost as far as my father could. My first fishing pole was an incredibly long one-piece bamboo number with an askew pigtailed tip, of the kind one used to pick out of bristling stacks that stood in front of hardware stores—your choice, fifteen cents. For I had bait fished many years before I graduated to the decadent luxury of having one of the new steel rods that magically tele-scoped, the kind my early fly-fishing hero Tommy Cole scornfully called a "collapsible girder."

In a canny effort to make myself indispensable so I'd never be left behind on fishing trips, I also contrived to become something of a neighborhood authority on the collection, preservation, and transportation of all man-ner of live baits, a dark art in which my father early schooled me. Though I haven't fished any kind of live bait in many years, I still remember most of those I gathered for my father and his fishing pals: chiefly an-gleworms and night crawlers, of course, and then a more esoteric and sometimes seasonal variety that included bloodsuckers, minnows, snaillike whitish things called grubs, and let's see, oh yes, grasshoppers and helgra-mites, to name the main ones.

I also learned that each species called for a special stalking and storing technique: night crawlers, as their name suggests, came much faster at night after a shower, especially when stalked like a footpad with a hooded-beam kerosene lantern with a sliding door (before flash-lights became common) of the kind refined ladies would today doubtless give their eyeteeth to get hold of to plant ivy in. My father also taught me that these crawlers, usually kept in a tub of rich black earth, became so

2

python lively they would even avidly grab a reluctant trout if, the night before your next fishing trip, you cagily transferred the trip's supply into a container of damp caribou moss.

Grasshoppers were best gathered before sunup, I soon learned, when the lively devils were still numb from the chill of night. These were clapped into a wooden bait box with a screen at one end and a sliding door at the other which my father fashioned out of old cigar boxes from his saloon. Then there were homemade minnow traps that one transferred to tricky buckets one was forever changing the water in. And there were the jars within jars for luring bloodsuckers, baited with liver, both a procedure and prey which gave me the creeps.

I pretty well stuck to garden worms and crawlers in my own fishing but my father played the field, using all the baits I've mentioned and others I've doubtless forgotten. He also had a macabre passion for all kinds of "boughten" dead baits, which I also failed to share (probably for economic as well as esthetic reasons), and he was a monthly pushover for the startling variety of pickled and embalmed baits that used to adorn the outdoor magazines, and still may.

A few years ago while I was rummaging through some of my father's old fishing gear I came up with a nostalgic prize: a bottle of what looked like the coveted remains of somebody's operation for tapeworms. Closer inspection of the faded label revealed that I was the proud inheritor of a virginal jar of pickled pork rind peddled by one of the early folk heroes of preserved baits, Al Foss. If any museum of ancient fishing tackle is interested, I'll cheerfully entertain bids . . .

3

My father had one hell of a time trying to switch from bait-fishing to fly-fishing, and he never made it. His youngest son also had one hell of a time making the switch, and he barely made it. My father's first discernible impulse to switch occurred when one of the earliest fly-fishermen I can remember moved to our town from the East. His name was August Ludington and he managed the local Singer Sewing Machine store—that is, when he managed to resist going out fishing with my father. I tagged along on their very first trip to our South Camp and there witnessed another fisherman fishing rings around my father. It was a rare spectacle.

To make it all the more humiliating, this feat took place on Blair Pond, one of my father's and my very favorite brook trout waters (also the setting of one of my earliest fishing stories, "Fishermen at Night," in case anybody gives a damn), though it was Mr. Ludington's first visit. I suppose what happened was that an evening fly hatch had come along and the trout were feeding far above my father's inert and ignored gob of worms. It was a lesson I never forgot, and in later years I used to wince when I saw the trout start "jumping" (as we crude bait heavers called it), because this told me they would henceforth pretty much ignore any bottom-fished bait, dead or alive.

Back up at camp I went into my lantern-lit fish-cleaning act, and I still recall my father's look of pained incredulity when, after he had dug a few wizened fish out of his giant wicker creel, Mr. Ludington calmly poured out an avalanche of glistening trout. My father's eyes bugged and his jaw fell and his lower lip trembled.

"Well I'll be goddamned," he said when he could

4

speak. "You mean you caught all *them* with a measly little fly that ain't even fit to eat?"

"That's right, George," Mr. Ludington said. "They were really on the prod tonight."

"My, my. Let's go have a drink—I guess I sorta need one."

When my fish-cleaning chores were done I got back into camp in time to make their third round of whiskey sours. I was also just in time to witness the event I'd all along been waiting for.

"Look, Lud," my father said as they clinked drinks, "where can a fella get hold of one of them there fly outfits?"

"Oh, Chicago or Milwaukee or almost any town back East."

"How much do they run?"

"Oh, twenty or thirty dollars should put you right in business, George."

"You mean the whole works—pole, reel, line—and some of them fake flies?"

"That's right, George, except we fly-fishermen call them *rods*, not poles."

"Hmm . . . Do you think you could get hold of an outfit for me?"

"Sure thing, George," Mr. Ludington said, glancing my way. "How about the youngster?"

"Nope, 'way too young for that there fancy new fangled fishing. How long will it take?"

"Should be here in a week, ten days," Mr. Ludington said, rising. "Here's bumps to the world's latest convert to fly-fishing."

"Thanks, Lud," my father said, glancing at me. "Step

5

lively and take the man's glass, son—can't you see it's empty? Might so well freshen mine up, too."

But the world's newest fly-fisherman never quite made the grade, as I've said. In fact his grotesque attempts were a disaster from the start, perhaps because his main motivation was wounded pride rather than any genuine feel for fly-fishing. I still have his antique fly outfit: an awesomely long and heavy rod made of ash, I believe; an old level silk line virtually time-glued to the corroded reel; and, the richest prize of the lot, a fat leather wallet full of snelled English flies of unfamiliar patterns, most of them never used, some of them still curled away in their parched soaking pads.

I recently went over these ancient treasures and, as I did, recalled some of the highlights of his gallant efforts to make the switch. Mr. Ludington tried valiantly to show him how to cast but my father could not seem to get it through his head that fly-casting was not a matter of brute strength but rather of rhythmic, purposeful timing. And since he was a big powerful man with a magnificently short fuse, sometimes he looked like a man trying to beat up the water into a lathered vat of his brewer father's choicest beer.

When Mr. Ludington was with us, out of pride my father pretty well stuck with his flies, but when we two were alone he'd often come sidling over and sheepishly mooch some worms off his youngest son. When the sad day finally came that Mr. Ludington had to move away all pretense fled: the fly outfit was reverently laid to rest, without flowers, and the collapsible girder permanently reappeared.

6

My own conversion to fly-fishing, if not quite so

dramatic or traumatic, was in some ways even more prolonged and uncertain. By this I do not imply that all older bait-fishermen are too soaked in sin ever to switch to fly-fishing; in fact, I know two notable proofs that it can be done if one really wants to. One is my old friend, the late L. P. "Busky" Barrett, who was past seventy when we taught him fly-casting; the other, a younger fishing pal, Anthony "Gigs" Gagliardi, was in his mid-forties when he made the switch, last summer further reddening our bourbon-flushed faces by catching the largest brookie of the lot.

Another advantage I had over my father was that by my mid-teens I began to feel a vague but growing disillusion with the *way* I was taking my trout. For one thing, I was getting weary of all the fuss and bother and uncertainty of gathering, preserving, and fishing with live bait. But mostly I felt an increasing distaste for the tied, inert, plunking quality of the way I was fishing compared with the dash and singing grace of men like Mr. Ludington.

But still I did not forsake bait-fishing, and after Mr. Ludington left town I kept doggedly plunking away, more out of inertia and lack of guidance than anything else, I suspect. By the time I was ready for college my fishing went into sort of an eclipse, my summers being largely devoted to selling everything under the sun—"Good day, Madam, may I please demonstrate the wondrous new housewife-emancipating Mother Goose self-wringing mop?"—and also celebrating my belated discovery that chasing girls was almost as much fun as chasing trout. But one day my schooling was over and I was back home again clutching my diploma and looking around for my old fishing gear.

7

I found it and shortly after that had the good fortune to meet Tommy Cole on a trout stream. I'd known about little old Tommy for years, of course, as one casually knows just about everyone in a small town. I knew him as one of the town's few dedicated native fly-fishermen as well as a bit of a choosy and aloof loner. Anyway, that day we fell to talking and discovered that both of us fished just about every day, so we made a date to go out together. We did, and hit it off from the start, and soon were fishing together almost daily.

As I look back on it, it seems both fitting and fateful that a chance meeting with a spunky fisherman on a remote trout stream not only changed my mode of fishing but in many ways, I suspect, my whole way of life. I'd now like to try to tell a little about this change and about the remarkable little man who inspired it.

2

Thomas Wellington Cole was a dark, slender little man of Cornish ancestry who had all the natural grace and gentility that as a boy I dreamed only dukes possessed. Though his formal education was both sketchy and brief, when he was not fishing or prowling the woods Tommy was an omnivorous reader and one of the most widely informed people I ever knew. Though I scarcely equate proficiency at word games with the highest cerebral flights, one of Tommy's more baffling feats was his ability regularly to solve the tough *New York Times* Sunday crossword without a dictionary, though I knew a fellow fisherman of his who couldn't even work the northwest corner of same with the help of five feet of encyclopedia.

As a young man Tommy also had a natural aptitude
for mechanics and, like many Upper Peninsula of
Michigan natives of that First World War era, was lured
to the Detroit area to work on Henry Ford's budding
assembly lines. Though he liked his job and the high
wages, he keenly missed his Lake Superior bush country.
When finally we got into the war to make the world safe
for democracy (which world, ironically, became more
and more totalitarian), Tommy promptly enlisted and
was sent to the front in France where, after much har-
rowing action, the Germans gassed him and he was ultimately shipped home. Since with his ravaged lungs he
could no longer do hard labor, he finally found a job in a
nearby town chauffeuring a country doctor.

This chance job opened up whole new fishing horizons
for Tommy, for it seemed that when Doctor Moll wasn't
delivering babies he was out in the brambles delivering
flies over trout. This was a daily ritual, in fact, and since
the old doctor took quite a fancy to little Tommy, he soon
initiated his new chauffeur into the art of fly-fishing and
even taught him to tie his own flies, including the Doctor
Trude fly, whose creator Tommy's doctor long knew and
had often fished with.

By the time I got to know Tommy the good doctor had
transferred his trout fishing to some pastoral celestial
realm and Tommy had returned home, resolved never
again to bear arms other than a fly rod. This resolve
included shunning all steady work and living on his
modest disability pension and going trout fishing every
day. By then I too was fishing almost daily, so we soon
joined forces and started going steady. And from the
very first day Tommy began a subtle campaign to wean

9

me away from bait-fishing and win me over to the fly—a rather large, uncertain undertaking as it finally turned out.

Tommy was that rare combination, a gentle man as well as a gentleman, and so he sensibly proceeded not by ridiculing and running down the way I fished, but by trying to make me see that fly-fishing was simply a vastly more exciting, artful, and humane way of wooing a trout. From the outset he conceded that in its way bait-fishing responded as much to patience and skill as did other forms of fishing—something I already ruefully knew from years of fishing with such wily bait foxes as Edward "Bud" Harrington and, later, Bill Gray, a real wizard with bait.

At the same time, Tommy kept pointing out that since the whole strategy of bait-fishing was to let the fish swallow the bait while the fly-fisherman, upon pain of instant rejection, had to strike his fish at once, in practice this meant that the mortality rate of returned bait-caught trout was virtually total, while that of fly-caught trout was virtually nil. The accuracy of Tommy's shrewd observation was borne out later by the field studies of my old fisheries friend, Al Hazzard (with whom I had much exciting fishing while he was still stationed in Michigan), and many others.

Tommy also quietly reminded me—as well as demonstrated almost daily—that the fly-fisherman was rarely plagued by catching such nongame fish as suckers and chubs and the like, though these trash fish were often the annoying bane of the bait-fisherman's existence. One evening after I'd caught such a monotonous procession

11

of stunted perch that I'd run clean out of worms and had to quit, Tommy squinted over my way for a spell, rubbing his chin, and finally spoke. "Look, pal," he said, "if you play your cards right and also promise to clean out my trout I'll be glad to rent you the fly I'm using for only half a buck."

"Go to hell, Cole," I said, folding my girder and sitting there morosely batting mosquitoes while Tommy played and deftly netted still another trout.

During these propaganda sessions, which ran the gamut from the needle to the bludgeon, Tommy also pointed out that though the common angleworm could often be a savage killer when the trout were bottom feeding, there were frequent periods during a fishing day, especially during a good fly hatch, when virtually all the trout were cruising and feeding at or near the top.

"During these periods," he once said, "a plunking bait-fisherman might just as well heave out a stillson wrench."

"Yes, I know," I said, remembering.

He also gently kept harping, and finally made me see, that for a fisherman to restrict himself to fishing the same lure all day—which is essentially what the bait-fisherman does—is as dull and boring and foolishly self-confining as an eccentric fly-fisherman who would regularly go fishing with but a single fly.

"Unless you're a commercial fisherman," he ran on, driving home his point, "the main aim and fun of going fishing at all is the action a guy gets, not the goddam fish—which, like as not, he'll either throw back or give away."

"Yes?" I said, listening closely.

"And as I think I've already shown you, chum, the best

12

way to get action trout fishing is to carry a varied assortment of flies—types, sizes, patterns—so that, if you're
lucky, you might finally toss out something they really
want." He widened his hands. "It's as simple as that,
pard—or do you still fail to see the light?"

"I do *see* it, Tommy," I once all but wailed, probably
while threading on still another worm, "but I can't seem
to be able to convince myself that a hungry trout will
continue to spurn something that's good to eat in prefer-
ence for grabbing a bare hook adorned with assorted
fluff that's fake and no good." I sighed, groping for
words. "It seems you're making me a fly-fisherman in my
head, Tommy, but not yet in my heart."

"That will come," Tommy solemnly promised.

A whole season passed this way, and part of the next,
with Tommy eloquently preaching the gospel of fly-
fishing while I kept doggedly pelting out my "pork
chops"—Tommy's scornful generic term for all live bait.
Along about mid-season of the second year Tommy
seemed to take a new tack: he talked less about the joys
and advantages of fly-fishing and instead seemed bent
on demonstrating them. Meanwhile, I wondered
whether he'd given up on me or was instead trying to
shame me into the paths of virtue. Whatever he had in
mind, one thing rapidly became clear—almost daily he
monotonously beat hell out of me fishing.

It must have been sometime around mid-August (this
was before I started keeping daily fishing notes) that
Tommy got a tip from a retired fishing pal that there
used to be some fabulous late-summer brown fishing on
a certain remote stretch of the upper reaches of the
Bogdan River, somewhere above the third wooden
bridge, and that maybe the place was still worth a shot.

13

Our own fishing was in a bit of a late-season slump, so the next afternoon we threw my little cedar boat on top of the old Model A (which the tipster had said was needed to reach the place), and headed for the third wooden bridge to have a look. Once there we quickly unloaded the boat and hid the Model A (against the prying eyes of rival fishermen) and were soon pushing our way upstream, using canoe paddles for oars.

We swiftly saw that Tommy's informant was at least partly right: the place was indeed isolated and hard to reach and, after a half-mile or so of maneuvering our way between the lush growth of overhanging tag alders, I was about ready to drown Tommy's tipster, having already accumulated quite enough material to write two books about all the phony fishing tips I'd followed.

Then came a spell of faster and shallower water, during which we several times had to get out and pull the boat, then a long stretch of more depressing tag alders. Then, rounding a slow bend, we came upon a wide, deep, open stretch, really an enormous pool, bounded on both sides by grassy natural meadows—"My friend says the Finnish farm kids used to swim here," Tommy explained—and suddenly we were beholding one of the most spectacular rises of big trout I've seen anywhere, before or since.

"Head her inshore," Tommy tensely whispered, and, once beached, we grabbed our gear and began rigging up with trembling hands. This was back in the gut leader and silk line days so, amidst all the plashing of big rising trout, meticulous Tommy had to go through the daily ritual of dressing out his line and scrubbing his leader

14

and all the rest while all I had to do was uncollapse my girder and impale a crawler on my harpoon and quick plop it in.

At least bait-fishing has one small advantage, I thought as I made my first plop, but this advantage rapidly waned. By the time Tommy was rigged up and ready, I had caught several wriggling chubs and one gasping sucker and was towing in another.

Tommy moved upstream a decent distance and made his first business cast as I was disimpaling my latest sucker. Almost instantly he was on to a tail-thwacking, rod-bending brown, which he quickly creeled. By the time my harpoon was freed and rebaited he had caught and returned two more lovely browns and was fast to another.

Doggedly I arose and flung a writhing new gob of crawlers far out into the steadily dimpling pool. Something grabbed it before my hook had settled and almost wrenched the girder out of my hands as it roared off and away, and I found myself engaged to a threshing tiger.

"It's a real *dandy*!" I hollered, bringing all my bait lore to the playing of my prize, my straining girder almost bent double, while Tommy held his fire and watched me land my epic fish.

"Boy oh boy!" I hollered, deftly thrusting my net under him (my sole concession to Tommy's way of fishing) and straining to hold high, for all the world to see, the slobbiest, yawpiest, most repellent sucker either of us had ever beheld. "Oh," I said in a small voice, abruptly sitting down. "Oh," I repeated, and then I just sat there, dully watching the crazily rising browns.

15

"If you'd only thought to bring your watercolors," Tommy said after a bit, "you could paint some mighty purty trout spots on it."

"Go to hell, Wellington," I murmured, on the verge of tears, heaving the mammoth sucker far back in the meadow.

Tommy reeled in and moved down my way and thrust out a supple, tanned hand. "Here," he said sharply, motioning with his fingers, "hand over that goddam girder."

"Yessir," I said, surrendering my treasure and watching him collapse and toss it clattering into the bottom of the boat.

"Take this," Tommy said, thrusting his precious fly rod out at me, "and go sit your ass in the front of the scow."

"Yessir," I said, automatically obeying.

"Tonight I'm going to make a fly-fisherman out of you," Tommy quietly vowed as he squatted in the stern and grabbed up a paddle, "or you'll never in hell ever make it."

"What d'you mean?" I said, bristling.

"Just what I said. Now shut up and pitch out that fly—without my good eye on it, if you'll please kindly try and manage that."

Before we left the pool I had busted off on two beauties and finally landed a third. Then in the gathering dusk Tommy slowly paddled me down through the narrow lane of tag alders, which by now seemed a boiling cauldron of threshing fish, during which I caught four more browns and lost some more of Tommy's flies, one lost brown seeming almost as large as an overfed water spaniel.

16

By the time we reached the third wooden bridge my little cedar boat carried a dedicated new convert to fly-fishing. "Tommy," I said, grabbing and pumping his hand when we landed, "thank you for turning your back on one of the most sensational trout rises we've ever seen, just to turn a stubborn bait-fisherman into a fly-fisherman. Tonight, my friend, you really made it and I thank you from the bottom of my heart."

"Cut out the corny sentiment," Tommy said gruffly, "and hold that bloody flashlight steady so a man can see to clean out these trout. Quit shaking, will you?"

"Yessir," I said, watching the kneeling, blurred figure of Tommy through the dancing columns of insects and trying to hold back my convulsive sobs of joy that tonight, thanks to this gallant little man, I was not only a fly-fisherman in my head but at last in my heart, the only place I guess it really matters.

2 Hemingway's Big Two-Hearted Secret

Once upon a time fishermen used to tie flies in winter to pass the time and help preserve a smidgin of sanity between seasons, but today more and more of them write books. And as this curious literary trend continues, all across the land I envision more and more littered tying benches being turned into writing desks as more and more of Mr. Mustad's hooks are forsaken for books. Things have reached such a pretty pass, my runners inform me, that some old tyers who turned from the dangling tying thread to the dangling participle have even stooped to *buying* their flies.

Of the loyal knot of diehards who still tie their own (augmented I suppose by a few jealous wordy ones stricken silent by writer's cramp) many seem to think that we literary types who prefer splitting our infinitives to tying our flies are, piscatorially speaking, faintly treasonable. This indictment is too sweeping, I think, because, taking my own case, I only turned to writing books when it became all too comically evident that nature had never endowed me for tying

flies but rather had left me so manually inept that, far from being able to tie a fly, I am barely able to unzip one.

Meanwhile the torrent of new fishing books continues, at last count exceeded only by those devoted to sex. And all that keeps the latter panting in a precarious lead—my sometimes still-shaken depth researchers inform me—is their greater abundance and stimulating variety of illustrations, both instructive and, one might say, inspirational. This may suggest that we fishermen possess a keener natural aptitude for wading than for wooing, besides possibly explaining why we can so readily get away.

All of which allows me to get *that* off my chest and down to paying my respects to one of the most powerful fishing stories I ever read—as well as possibly the most famous—written by one who must surely be the most famous of modern fisherman-writers. The story is "Big Two-Hearted River" written, of course, by Ernest Hemingway. Along the way I shall comment in my fashion on some side effects of this remarkable story as well as touch on some of the curious legends that have gathered round it.

Hemingway's story first appeared in the "little" magazine *This Quarter* and soon after in one of his earliest books, if not the earliest, first published in 1925 and called *In Our Time*. Since then the story has been widely reprinted in a procession of anthologies as well as endlessly dissected and explicated by what one awed beholder might call a whole new piscatorial school of academic writing inspired by the story—or should I say spawned?

The story's title comes, of course, from the name of an actual Upper Peninsula of Michigan trout stream called

19

the Two Hearted River, the maps I've seen omitting the author's Big and his hyphen between Two Hearted. Yet despite these small differences the connection between the story and the stream remains as obvious as it is undeniable. Moreover, as any fisherman knows, it is sound fisherman's idiom to call that portion of a river "big" beyond where its principal branches come together. Such a stretch of river in my own bailiwick, for example, is the Escanaba River below the village of Gwinn which, all unimaginative cartographers to the contrary, most local fishermen continue to call the "big" Escanaba.

When I first read Hemingway's story many years ago I had never so much as heard of the Two Heart (again sound fisherman's idiom), much less ever fished it; all this despite the fact that I was born and raised in the same Peninsula and had been trout fishing avidly almost from diaperhood. One explanation is that back in those days fishing was still so good almost everywhere that few fishermen needed to stir far beyond their own backyards to get all the action they craved. In fact I can still remember—to my undying shame—bicycling out after school to a stream that today yields mostly beer cans, and getting home in time for supper sagging under the weight of my father's big wicker creel full of trout.

Today all that is changed and the once remote and obscure Two Hearted River has become a sort of combined literary shrine and tourist mecca. So crowded have grown the annual summer pilgrimages to the place, I am told, that a new campsite of the same name has sprung up nearby, as well as a landing strip, all to help accommodate the reverent throngs who annually flock there to trod the same ground and wade the same waters made famous by Nick Adams.

It's a clear case of a story making a river famous, much like the river Kwai, so famous in fact that steps are being taken to save the river from the clutches of those modern brigands (who, with our helpless passion for kidding ourselves, we ever so elegantly prefer calling developers) bent upon demonstrating their unappeasable hunger for literature by lining the river's banks with everything from prefabricated cardboard fishing "lodges" to sylvan trailer courts on down to canoe liveries and only God knows what else. What is happening to the Two Hearted River, in short, is enough to break a fisherman's heart.

Vying with the visiting fishermen and tourists is a steady stream of literary scholars (or wistful degree-seeking aspirants to that status) who, arriving with notebook in hand, quickly make up in articulateness whatever they lack in numbers. For, invariably following their summer pilgrimages, there presently flutters upon the world a new spate of annotated papers, inevitable as the falling snow, uncovering brand-new layers of neglected symbolism found lurking in Nick's story as well as usually unveiling still another route he took to get from Seney to his Shangri-La.

Not that all of these scholars agree, heaven knows, for on many points they disagree, sometimes rather violently. And while I have barely scratched the surface of the vast literature on the subject, from the little I've read I quickly learned that when scholars get hot under the collar mere fishermen had better not get caught in the crossfire of their footnotes. A small heretical band of these scholars has even reached conclusions not too far from mine, though mostly for other reasons.

21

By far the greater bulk of these papers assume that Nick Adams must have fished the Two Hearted River because the author used that name in his title. Their disagreements (aside from an endless quibbling over the kind and significance of the symbolism they continue to find) are limited largely to what route Nick took from Seney to the river, which they delight in endlessly re-retracing.

Some have bayed and beagled along after Nick so diligently that they claim to have tracked down the precise spot above that dense cedar swamp where Nick did his thing. But even here they disagree so widely that about all they've proved, to me at least, is what a hell of a lot of swamps there must be on the Two Heart. The main pitch of my piece, then, is not so much to show where Nick did fish as possibly to show that these pro-Two Heart scholars just might be barking up the wrong river.

I first read Hemingway's "Big Two-Hearted River" so long ago I must still have been in school. It affected me deeply then, both as an aspiring writer and as a fellow fisherman, as it still does. Always I am especially moved by the reverence for place, for unspoiled nature, the story shows, as though Nick were visiting—or, more accurately, revisiting—some cherished shrine. And upon each reading, too, I am again moved by the power and intensity of the author's recapture of mood: the pent and yet almost heart-bursting ecstasy of the lone fisherman who has reached a truce with his world and, for a time-stopped interlude, finds it good.

Then, too, I've always admired the sure intimate knowledge of the ways of wild trout the story shows, which can't be faked. Above all I continue to envy and marvel over the author's way with the simple declarative sentence: the high emotional charge he contrives to pack into it, and, as his sentences march along, their strange incantatory effect, their beguiling hypnotic beat, as though they were being hammered out on some invisible anvil. What all this eruption of critical rhetoric adds up to, I guess (besides possibly showing a recent overexposure to certain scholarly papers), is that Hemingway's "Big Two-Hearted River" has long been and remains one of the most haunting and memorable stories I've ever read.

Having said all that it seems a shame, as well as a trifle disloyal, to have to confess that I have never yet visited the Two Hearted River, much less ever cast a fly upon its waters. The reasons I haven't cut to the heart of my discourse are as few as they are simple. First, like most far-gone fishermen, I've more and more shunned all crowded waters as I've more and more discovered that when one is trout fishing sometimes even two can be a crowd while anything over three is a milling throng.

But that cannot be the main reason, because the truth is I've never really wanted to fish the river, even back in the days before the thundering multitude moved in. And the reason I never wanted to was simply because it never occurred to me that the Two Hearted River could possibly be the water Hemingway had in mind when he wrote his story. So fisherman's pride is involved, too, for how can any fisherman feeling as I do possibly make a worshipful trek to the Two Heart and thus not only show himself a hypocrite but at the same time proclaim to the world how badly he's misread both the story and its author?

23

In saying this I must quickly add that I am not trying to start a donnybrook with the pro-Two Heart scholars or even mildly to tease or twit them. In fact I rather envy them all the fun and footnotes they keep dredging up out of one lone story . . . not to mention all those layers of symbolism. Rather, as a fisherman, it both comforts and charms me to think that the more tourists and fishermen and fellow scholars their effusions keep luring to the Two Heart the longer will be spared the actual waters Hemingway had in mind. All I seek is equal time, as the saying goes, on the democratic theory that if so many of our literary scholars can keep telling me where Nick Adams must have fished, perhaps one cantankerous old fisherman may hazard his own guess where maybe, goddammit, he didn't.

That guess then, to spell it out, is that whatever water the author may have had in mind when he wrote his story, almost certainly it was *not* the Two Hearted River. And in making this guess I am placing no reliance whatever upon the rather considerable evidence to that effect in the story itself, some of which I'll touch on anyway just for the hell of it and maybe also to flash my fisherman's erudition.

Thus, for a starter, nowhere in the story does Hemingway name the water Nick Adams fished; that sole authorial clue comes only from the title. But if *that* is the main proof of the pro-Two Heart forces then it must be equally true that Nick left his train at the village of Seney because this time the author tells us so in the body of the story, for good measure throwing in a moving description of the place, so recently scarred and scorched by forest fires.

"Quick, Watson, my maps!" I would shout at this juncture, triumphantly pointing out that Seney is not only in a different county from the Two Heart but many miles west of where any even faintly savvy fisherman would leave his train were he hiking there.

A real stinkeroo would next point out that Nick must have toted an awesome pack load clear from Seney to wherever he fished, and all in the same day, because again the author tells us so. He would then tick off just some of the contents of that historic pack: three blankets, one canvas tent, a coil of rope, assorted canned goods, a bag of nails, towels and toilet articles, buckwheat pancake flour, one frypan, a wire grill, a coffee pot, one hand ax—besides a leather rod case and his other fishing gear. Croaking with triumph, he would then point out that anyone making even a packless hike in one day from Seney to the Two Heart's nearest branch would need to be a modern Paul Bunyan, and that if he further aspired to hit it where it became "big," as I earlier defined it, he would have hiked almost up to Lake Superior.

Finally, twirling his mustache and flourishing his maps, El Stinko would show that the closest railroad stop to the Two Hearted River was and remains the town of Newberry; that Newberry is at least twenty-five miles east of Seney and thus that much closer for Nick to have detrained (since he says he came north by way of St. Ignace); and, finally, that while no stream of consequence flows through or near Newberry (remember Nick watching the darting shadows of those lovely trout in a nearby river soon after leaving his train?), the imposing West Branch of the Fox River still flows through the Seney loop.

25

Indeed, if one's concern were to show where Nick might have fished rather than where he didn't, a strong case could be made for it being somewhere on the upper reaches of the Fox within decent packing distance of Seney. (Nick several times says he hiked northerly from Seney and hit the river by bearing left, whereas the Two Heart would simply have to be many miles to his *right*.) But I will not press the point for several reasons, one of them being that I haven't the slightest illusion that anything I can say here would now measurably divert any traffic away from the Two Heart. Another is that, as a fisherman, I wouldn't want to if I could. Why, I would guiltily ask myself, why should anyone risk opening up still another tourist stamping ground trying to save a stricken stream already beyond hope?

For the really sad truth of the matter, and one that I am sure would deeply pain the author if he knew it out there, is that by now the poor invaded Two Hearted River is so mired in the national mythology and so glued to the tourist beat that even a posthumous disavowal by the author himself probably wouldn't save it. And *that*, if true, may be a comfortless parable for our time.

To any die-hard Two Hearter still tempted to argue that maybe the author had his railroad stops mixed when he later wrote his story in Paris, probably without maps, a fisherman could reply that he's rarely known another fisherman who forgot the way to a memorable spot. Especially would this be so, he might add, if that fellow fisherman had shown so strongly in both his writing and his own fishing and hunting such a sure sense of place and pride of woodcraft.

No, if any ambiguity does exist in the story about

26

An early snapshot of Ernest Hemingway (in cap on right) and visiting companion from Oak Park, Illinois, ready for an overnight pack-in trip in Michigan. The reverse side of the photograph bears this scribbled legend: "Lewis Clarahan & Ernie enroute to the Fox River." This old photo is owned and a copy was generously provided by Hemingway's sister and Robert Traver's friend, Mrs. E. J. ("Sunny" Hemingway) Miller of Petoskey, Michigan.

where Nick Adams might have fished—and only the
most dogged pro-Two Hearter would deny that—then it
seems almost surely to have been planted there deliberately by its author. If so, the conclusion seems inescapa-
ble that it was not done simply to furnish fuel to future
scholars but rather to throw the canaille off the scent and
help protect and save the real place Nick had fished.

But for me to depend on the story itself to prove where
Nick Adams did or didn't fish is to play the scholar's
game; my "evidence" is simpler, less demonstrable and, I
must face it, far more subjective if not plain mystical. The
one big reason I feel so sure Nick Adams wasn't fishing
the Two Heart is, as I've already hinted, that I know that
the author was since boyhood an experienced and savvy
trout fisherman.

In support of this I know from a variety of sources that
when he wrote his story in Paris in the early 1920s,
Hemingway was still an ardent inland-water trout
fisherman, this still being several years before he was
struck by the twin lightning bolts of fame and fortune
and graduated to deep-sea fishing. (Those too puzzled
or pained by this switch are free to put quotes around
that "graduated.") Finally, I can offhand recall few writ-
ers whose work and life pattern more clearly reveal a
man who lived by a strict personal code, one rivaling even
that of us helplessly ritualistic and taboo-ridden trout
fishermen, which of course he also was.

Once a fisherman knows these things about a fellow
fisherman the rest is easy. First, he knows in his bones
that such a man is never going to snitch on any water he
truly loves, least of all in writing. He further knows that if
his author does name an actual stream or whatnot, it is

27

only to fool and divert the multitude away from the real place he has in mind; either that or the water he does name, usually a river, is so big and long and meandering and so many-feedered and be-branched and so full of dams or boulders or swamps or unwadable or fishless bald spots that any stranger would need a guide to find a hot spot.

Such a tantalizing river is the lovely meandering Escanaba arising in my own bailiwick—accurately named, I must say, in what is possibly my own most reprinted fishing story, "The Intruder"—and winding up in distant Lake Michigan more than a hundred river-miles away, precisely the kind of vast anonymous stream that even a glance at a map shows the Two Heart isn't.

Finally it strikes this fisherman as requiring no very profound insight to guess that the author of "Big Two-Hearted River"would no more publicly expose the identity of his own precious trout water (and his story reverberates with the feeling of *that*) than he would that of an adored woman he'd slept with. Putting it most bluntly, then, far from drawing any pro-Two Heart proof from the author's use of that name in his title, I take it as the final clinching proof that, of all the trout waters in the area, it could not possibly have been *that* stream. Once this point is reached the conclusion seems inevitable that if brother-fisherman Hemingway ever fished the Two Hearted River the only thing he found memorable about it was its romantic-sounding offbeat name.

3 Is There a Mermaid in Your Creel?

Fly-fishing is such great fun, I have often felt, that it really ought to be done in bed. Not that high frolic is the only thing the pursuit of fish and the pursuit of females have in common; these ancient sports have more going for them than that—as I'll now try to tell why.

First off, just as both diversions are best conducted in decent privacy, away from distracting crowds, so too the most gratifying results are best obtained by subtlety rather than by force, by seduction rather than by rape.

Again, just as both pastimes quickly pall when the conquest is too easy, so too the lures used in the wooing, whether jewels or Jassids, must be presented with the utmost skill and grace.

Still again, just as in both endeavors the exact nature of one's presentation is best kept disguised until the moment of truth, so in both the thrilling moment of submission is preceded by the fiercest resistance and followed by the sweetest fatigue.

Yes, and just as fishermen are the only children I know who can celebrate Christmas every day all summer long, so too can the roving romancer visit new pastures every day—provided both possess the stamina and stomach to stand it.

Both types crave variety in the quarry sought, just as they do in the size and pattern of their enticements, in which latter area both tolerantly pursue the policy of "fishing the waters."

Mercifully we shall not dwell on the assorted sparrings and perspirings and slippings and fallings and comic collidings that inevitably accompany both pursuits, just as we can only barely salute the game fish and the game gal as two of nature's loveliest creations.

Finally, just as the aging fisherman and the sagging lover boy can one day only dream of the fabled ones that got away, so too both can later muse with an old man's secret smile over those that didn't.

4 *A Flick of the Favorite Fly*

'Twas the night before Christmas when all through the house not a sound could be heard above the interminable caroling and trilling over the radio about some freespending lover boy who kept pelting his adored with the damndest assortment of Christmas junk I ever heard of, winding up with, of all things, a partridge in a pear tree —for which coveted yuletide prize, as anybody knows who's ever owned one, she must surely have long been panting. Then the phone rang and I gratefully dove for it.

"Michigan's mightiest piscator," I said, prolonging the first syllable of the last word beyond any shred of decency, thinking the call was from one of my local fishing pals.

"Merry Christmas, mighty fisherman," a strange voice said. "This is Art Flick."

"Oh, I'm so sorry, Mr. Flick," I mumbled contritely, feeling my ears burning. "I thought you were one of the local boys I fish with. We carry on that way."

"*What's that?*"

"I mean I thought you were somebody else . . . What I mean is I didn't mean to sound so braggy . . . Oh hell . . . Merry Christmas to you, Mr. Flick. You must have got my letter about your book."

"Yes, my publisher just forwarded it, hence the delay in thanking you. So tonight on an impulse I thought I'd phone and say hello and tell you how tickled I am to get such a nice fan letter from the author of *Trout Madness*, which I too greatly enjoyed. That makes us even."

"Not quite," I said, "because I write only in winter, while you sacrificed three whole summers of fishing to gather the dope for your book. Your book is based on solid fact while some of my more caustic critics call my fishing tales my best fiction. You wrote your book the hard way while I suspect that if I could always have fished all winter I'd probably never have written a line."

"You're making me purr," my caller said, chuckling. "I also wanted to tell you I'm thinking of accepting your kind invitation to come out your way fishing."

"*Now?*" I shrilled, glancing out at the windrows of drifted snow that almost reached our windowsills.

"Scarcely," Art said. "Probably not till late June or early July, depending upon the water level of my own Schoharie, which usually gets pretty low about then."

"Simply wonderful," I said. "I don't mean about your favorite river pooping out but about your coming out here fishing."

"*What's that?*"

"I mean how would you plan coming?"

"I'll probably drive and come by way of Canada so I can maybe stop and fish any likely spots I see along the way. My maps show Canada may be the shortest route."

"I think it is," I said, "and surely more pastoral. I believe you cross over near Buffalo and repatriate in Michigan almost within casting range of my back door."

"Your three minutes are up," the operator chimed in—which may furnish some small clue about how many Christmases ago our deathless conversation took place.

My caller took the hint, clearing his throat for a quick farewell. "Well then," he said, "I'll be seeing you next summer if all goes well."

"Great. And I'll be rereading your book and making up a list of trouty spots for us to hit. Merry Christmas."

"Happy New Year," Art Flick said, varying the formula. "Until next summer, then, good-bye."

After hanging up I strained to hear that clucking partridge in his pear tree but, lo, he'd gone to roost. I longed to follow him there but felt I ought to wait up to see that Santa did not get himself stuck crossways in our chimney while delivering that new fly rod I'd so thoughtfully helped him pick out.

Meanwhile, I reached for a slender volume lying on my reading table. It was called *Art Flick's Streamside Guide to Naturals and Their Imitations,* the book that had smoked out my first fan letter ever. And since Santa as usual was running late, there seemed no time like the present to start my refresher course. So I turned to Chapter One, "Selectivity of Trout," and read on and on until, with a jolly ho-ho-ho, Santa suddenly dropped in and broke it up—my reading, I mean, not that fragile split-bamboo fairy wand he kept waving about.

The big thing I liked about Art Flick's little book was that at one stroke it had brought order out of the prevailing chaos of flies and fly patterns. Naturally I had tried

33

many times to dispel the mystery by reading large esoteric tomes on this murky subject. But by the time the love life of the hundredth fly was revealed, pinned down, and identified, both in English and in Latin, the sedative effect became so overwhelming I sometimes had to be shaken awake. Since I couldn't ever seem to remember a hundred fly patterns, I usually compromised by remembering none.

This is the common lot of a surprising number of fly-fishermen, I'd guess—even those who've written nostalgic fairy tales about their passion—many of whom would be lucky to be able to name even a tenth of the patterns that lurk among the neglected forests of flies they cart around, much less hazard a guess what naturals they are supposed to imitate. Overnight, Art's book changed all that.

The man had done this by the simple expedient of cutting to the bone the number of working mayfly patterns he felt any sane fisherman needed to carry. To learn what these were he had devoted three summers to prowling his beloved Schoharie in upstate New York armed only with an insect net and pickling bottles—catching, sorting, and ruthlessly weeding out.

Most of the scores of species he finally rejected lost out because Art felt their hatches were either too seldom or too small or too fleeting or too nocturnal or a combination of these. When he'd boiled down the survivors to less than a dozen he tied up his own imitations of this small elite, furnishing sketches and photos of both as well as charts of their average annual emergence dates, and called the result simply *Streamside Guide*.

That winter, besides working on a new fishing book of

34

my own, I read and reread Art's book several times. And each time I marveled over how any fisherman could possibly possess not only the stamina but the awesome character to be able to quit fishing cold for three seasons running simply to chase bugs, no matter how helpful the results might be to his slothful fellow fishermen who so merrily fished away their own summers. Like a small boy learning his ABCs, I learned by heart all the popular names of Art's selected patterns—Quill Gordon and all the rest—getting so carried away that I even took to mispronouncing their scientific Latin names.

"March Brown," I'd chant my way down the list, intoning their Latin equivalents with the sonority of a cardinal. "*Stenonema vicarium!*" When in late June a note came from Art that he was just taking off and would probably arrive by the afternoon of the twenty-ninth his zealous Midwest disciple was all primed and ready.

Several droll coincidences attended the arrival of Arthur B. Flick. One was that it so happened another fishing pal was already visiting me, photographer Bob Kelley of *Life* magazine, who had flown in to work on the final layout of our own forthcoming word-and-picture book, *Anatomy of a Fisherman*, since duly published but now long out of print, alas.

Bob thought he needed a few more "snaps" for our book, and since the twenty-ninth dawned with a rare total overcast we decided over breakfast to make a quick dash out to Frenchman's Pond in my jeep and get our pictures and thus be rid of all distracting chores by the time Art arrived.

The occasion also happened to be my birthday, but this macabre circumstance failed to dampen our spirits as the

35

jeep dropped off the edge of the last improved road with a thump and began bouncing its way over an endless series of jack pine roots lying exposed in the sandy ruts. As the trees grew larger and more plentiful the bouncing became so frequent and violent that our talk became a kind of breathless stutter.

"Wa-wa-what's that?" Bob inquired as we felt a sudden definitive jolt in the rear of the jeep, which grated to an abrupt stop as we sat curiously watching a lone automobile wheel go languidly bouncing past in a cloud of dust and head gracefully for the woods.

"I'm afraid that, Robert," I said wearily, "is a rear tire and wheel off the vehicle we are—or rather were—riding in."

"What do we do?" Bob said when, after searching among the tall ferns, we finally retrieved the wayward wheel—including also, I pensively noted, a rusted brake drum from which peeked a small gleaming section of broken axle.

"We flip a coin," I sighed and said, "to see who hoofs it to hell out to the nearest phone to call a goddam wrecker."

Bob held out for cribbage, a game he'd monotonously been taking me at since his arrival, but fortune smiled and I won, which so relieved me that the new cribbage champ fixed Bob a king-sized belt of bourbon to speed him on his way, pouring one for himself for company.

"I'll phone your Grace, too, so she'll know what's cooking," Bob said, downing his drink and shedding the last of his cameras and starting off on his long dusty march.

36

"Give her my love," I called after him, shivering a little over the prospect of the domestic lecture this latest calamity would surely win me over the mounting cost of keeping my fish car ambulant.

It was nearly noon before Bob got back with Olaf the wrecker man, having sensibly waited for him at the roadside tavern from which he'd phoned and where both had obviously tarried to celebrate my birthday. After a few more rounds of birthday drinks Olaf spat on his hands and backed his wrecker up to the rear of the jeep and soon had it dangling from high aloft.

"All aboard!" Olaf leaned out his cab and hollered. "Ever'body yump in."

So Bob clambered aboard and I made as though to follow. "Only vun fella rides oop hare vit me," Olaf announced, holding up a warning hand.

"How come?" I said.

"Sompbody's got to ride in da yeep," he explained. "Ay clean forgot to brung dem goldang front-wheel towing bars, so Ay guess you gotta steer da ting."

"I see," I said, and somehow managed to scale my dangling jeep and wrestle my way behind the wheel. "Toot, toot an' avay ve goo!" I hollered out my window, suddenly falling into the Viking spirit of the thing.

Naturally over the years I've arrived home from fishing in a rather wide variety of states and positions, but the day I met Art Flick was the very first time I ever made it there backward. As Olaf slowed down for the turn into his employer's garage I glanced out at the knot of curious on-lookers and saw my wife, Grace, standing next to a strange man.

"Hi, Grace," I hollered. "Who's your handsome escort?"

"Your expected guest, Mr. Flick," she called back.

37

"He's only been waiting around since shortly after you and Bob took off after breakfast."

"Sorry," I said as we rolled on into the garage and Olaf thoughtfully brought up a ladder so I could more quickly dismount and go greet my neglected fishing guest.

As Art Flick and I shook hands I saw a tall, tanned, crew-cut man who, although I knew we were virtually the same age, possessed the shy, diffident smile of a growing boy. After introducing Bob I tried to explain what had happened.

"Forget it," Art said, looking up at the lovely persisting overcast. "Fisherman's luck. Anyway, I wrote you not to expect me so early. Who's for going fishing?"

"Hm . . ." I said, reflectively rubbing my chin and eyeing my wife's shiny new sedan. "Hm . . . "

"We'll take my old crate," Art said, swiftly appraising the brewing domestic crisis. "You boys go get your fishing gear while I clear out some space."

"Good-bye," I called out to Grace as we three rolled off; and she bravely waved us on our way and, I think, even managed a little smile.

2

One of the first rules in fishing is that there are few rules in fishing that resourceful trout do not manage to break. Indeed, if there be any they don't smash to smithereens at one time or another my top candidate is this one: if you want to make sure the fishing will turn lousy, just dare invite a fellow angler from far away; the farther, the lousier. Before the poor man's visit is over you can lay ten to one you'll be muttering some version of

38

the classic lament of Pierre the Guide, "Mistaire, you shoulda been 'ere las' week."

Then, ah yes, there's that companion rule I almost forgot. The moment your fishless guest takes off the fishing will magically improve. This too I've seen happen so many times I've adopted an Italian switch on Pierre's old refrain.

It was taught me by an early fishing pal, priceless Luigi "Calla-me-Louie" Bonetti, an unreconstructed bait-fisherman who was forever luring me to join him on epic cross-country hikes into fabled fishing spots that often as not turned out to be either (a) nonexistent, or (b) fly-fishable only from a tethered balloon, or (c) just plain lousy.

On one such memorable day we'd slogged and hewn our way in so far that I felt like *both* Lewis and Clark. At last Louie paused on a ridge and pointed down in triumph at a shallow malarial puddle from which we proceeded to extract an endless procession of wriggling chubs. When exhaustion and disillusion finally made us both sit down in order to gather ourselves for the long hike out, Louie the eternal optimist tried to comfort me.

"My frien'," he declaimed, reaching over and patting my sweat-dampened shoulder, "you shoulda been 'ere *anexa* week!"

And so it was during the visit of Arthur Flick. We two fished morning, noon, and night. We fished rivers and streams and we fished ponds and beaver dams. We fished alone and we fished with others, including such wily local fly-fishing hands as Hank Scarffe and Bill Nault. But nothing helped, of course, for the visitor's hex was firmly glued upon the week.

39

During his six-day stay I don't think Art and I between us caught a dozen decent trout. In fact I know we didn't because my daily fishing notes, which I've kept since Depression days, tell the whole sad story. Here is a typical entry. "Another day of fruitless flailing, this on the beautiful stretch around Seem's Rock below the Hoist Dam. Bob Kelley sensibly gave up and took off this A.M. Art loved the water and gave it the old college try, but around 6:00 P.M. we got abruptly washed out by an advancing tidal wave as the goddam kilowatt boys began running their goddam dam. Maybe better luck tomorrow."

And so it went day after day until, in desperation, I personally guided Art to the very hottest spot in the very hottest fishing place I knew—the old beaver dam on Frenchman's Pond.

"Arthur," I said, pointing at a calm, inky stretch lying between the two gurgling outlets and shaded and protected by clumps of overhanging bushes, "this is the hottest spot in the whole pond as well as the deepest. It is also one of the toughest spots to cast a fly," I ran on, feeling like a realtor trying to peddle the place, "which probably explains why it holds such lovely brooks."

"Hm," Art said as I paused for breath, at the same time quietly appraising his best casting position.

"Bottom's a vast tangle of crossed logs," I continued, this time pausing only to grope for more adjectives. "Favorite hiding place of some of the most gorgeous native brook trout I've seen anywhere. Go get 'em, Arthur."

40

The sun had emerged during my declamation, so while we waited for more cloud cover I got my second

wind and proceeded to give Arthur a free lecture on the
desirability of using wee flies and fine leaders on this
particular pond. I found the courage to dare counsel the
sage of the Schoharie because I'd been haunting the
pond for at least a hundred years during which, as I told
him, I had yet to behold a hatching insect larger than a
wizened split pea.

Art listened gravely to my further spurts of piscatorial
wisdom, nodding occasionally as enlightenment
dawned. By the time I was done the sun had again gone
under so, aglow with virtue over my burst of unselfish-
ness, I withdrew out of range and gave Art the stage. "Go
get 'em, Arthur," I repeated.

Arthur wasted no time, already feeding out line, and
as his undulant casts gradually lengthened I had the
illusion he was whipping a small bird back and forth.
"*Wheep, wheep!*" chirped the screaming birdie as I stood
pondering its possible breed.

"Arthur," I whispered hoarsely, "what in hell kind of
fly *are* you using?"

"Oh, a little something I happened to have on," he
whispered back, keeping his eye on the ball. "Just
thought I'd give it a quick try before switching to the
small stuff."

Suddenly it occurred to me that I'd recently heard this
same soaring creature somewhere before, especially
when none of Art's other patterns happened to be hatching. Then came the shock of recognition.

"You mean your Grey Fox Variant?" I whispered, my
heart sinking, for this was probably his biggest pattern,
something akin to pelting out a swooping condor, say,
compared with the minute flies I'd just been extolling.

41

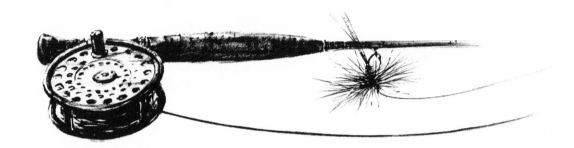

"Right-o," Art replied, raising his arm high for the final delivery. "Happens to be a real favorite of mine . . . sorta like those wee babies are with you."

"*Ephemera guttulata*," I murmured, all but kneeling and crossing myself as Arthur released his cast.

I watched, frozen, as the line raced far out over the waiting dam like a lash, seeming for an instant to hang suspended over the magic spot, then the leader sleepily folding over and forward and the fly slowly drifting down on target with the dreamy languor of a falling leaf.

There was the sudden flash as of a shaft of lightning as a great dripping creature rose and in one savage roll engulfed Art's favorite fly. The canny fisherman struck, gently but firmly, and I winced my eyes shut as I heard the faint telltale *ping* that shouted to the world that my friend Arthur had just been cleaned out by the most glorious trout we'd beheld all week.

"*Wowie!*" Art hollered, grinning from ear to ear. "I see what you mean."

"Anyway, I was half right," I said. "There *was* a big one there—even if he was dumb enough to hit your feather duster."

"Think I'll rest the spot and try another," Art announced, flipping open a large fly box to expose what looked like a whole nodding field of feather dusters.

"Think I'll mosey along upstream," I said, after morosely watching him tie on an exact duplicate of the fly he'd just lost.

"Don't take 'em all," Arthur ritually said, carefully testing the new fly against the leader as I shook my head and silently moved away.

"Art," I said, suddenly turning back, all pride flown,

43

"you wouldn't happen to have an extra *guttulata* on you you could spare a pal, would you?"

"Sure thing," Art said, tossing me his big fly box. "But there's one thing you've got a little wrong."

"What's that?" I said, making a flying catch.

"Actually, it's the Green Drake that's called *Ephemera guttulata*," he went on, feeding out line, "a fly I've personally found most difficult to tie a decent imitation of."

"My, my," I said, reciprocal enlightenment dawning.

"And while the large Grey Fox Variant doesn't really imitate the Green Drake—or indeed anything for that matter—it's a mighty good attracter fly that I've also found can be a darned effective substitute when the natural is hatching." He paused in his fly-casting and cast me a quick smile. "In fact it often works, I've found, when the Green Drake *isn't* hatching."

"So I've noticed," I said, prying open his aluminum treasure chest.

"Just help yourself and leave the box there," Art said, intent on his casting. "Carry 'em by the dozen. Favorite fly, you know."

"Sorta sweeps over me," I murmured as I snitched a couple of Art's feather dusters and moved upstream toward another likely spot. But the spell was broken and though we faithfully flailed away until hunger and dusk reprieved us, neither of us saw or raised another trout that could hold even a candle to the glorious one Art had earlier made love to and lost.

3

Though I wouldn't go so far as to say that I fish to improve my mind, I do think I learned a lot while fishing with Arthur Flick. In fact I suspect all fishermen learn something from every new fisherman, even from the clumsiest duffers. And Art Flick was no duffer, heaven knows, being one of the loveliest fishermen I've ever fished with, and there've been a few. By this I mean that not only was he a superb fly caster but, possibly even more important, an observant stalker, a careful hoarder of his casts, and a subtle and endlessly patient wooer of the elusive trout.

One of the biggest lessons I learned from Art, or possibly had confirmed, is that catching an occasional fish is to the enjoyment of trout fishing what encountering an occasional oyster is to the enjoyment of oyster stew: gratifying, yes, but far from everything. Poor as our fishing was in the things one could weigh and calibrate, we two had ourselves a ball.

There were several other little tricks and handy things I learned from Arthur, of course, just as he probably picked up a stray thing or two from me, these little exchanges being a sort of small currency of good will among kindred fishermen. But by all odds the most comforting lesson I learned from Arthur was this: that even the master himself, the man who tracked down and dreamed up his own creations, was himself a helpless slave to a favorite fly—even as you and I.

Why a fly becomes a favorite is about as profound a proposition to unravel, I'd guess, as Calvin Coolidge's historic revelation to a waiting nation that when a lot of people are out of work unemployment results. A fly becomes a favorite, of course, because the fisherman happened to have the damn thing on that memorable day when they would have probably as avidly hit an old carpet slipper. Either that or, at the opposite extreme, he happened to have the "right" fly on during a highly selective feeding period and, moreover, happened also to have sneezed or tripped or something and thus given it just the right action at just the right moment . . .

Like a boy and his favorite toy, any fisherman naturally favors the fly he once had all that fun with. And fun to a fly-fisherman above all means getting action. The infatuation, you see, is cumulative: the more the fisherman fishes his favorite fly, inevitably the more favorite that fly becomes. It does so because naturally any fish he catches have simply *got* to be on it, but also because henceforth he fishes his favorite with greater confidence and extraloving care—two imponderable but sometimes crucial factors in that enchanting woodland gambol known as casting the fly. Or is that word spelled "gamble"?

A favorite among flies is like the reigning favorite in a harem: neither is likely to be soon displaced by those veiled and neglected rivals who so seldom get the boss man's nod. Or as Calvin himself might have put it, were he addicted to fisherman's idiom, flies that so resolutely remain hidden in one's fly box aren't ever apt to catch a hell of a lot of trout. And Calvin would have said a mouthful.

Came the final evening when our fun and frolic was over and the next morning Grace and I walked our guest out to his car to say good-bye.

"Arthur," I said, shaking hands, "I've just dreamed up a theory why our fishing was so lousy."

"What's that?" Arthur said—after six days, perhaps a little warily.

"I'm afraid our local trout are just plain illiterate," I said. "Since they haven't been able to read our books, naturally they couldn't know how good we are."

"I have a more comforting theory," Art said as he thoughtfully climbed into his car. "Your trout aren't illiterate at all and they've avidly read both our books."

"Yes?" I said, rising to the fly.

"Consequently they *do* know how good we are, so naturally when they saw us both together they simply fled in terror." He smiled his boyish smile. "Thanks for everything, you two, and good-bye."

"Arturo," I murmured after him as he rolled away, "you shoulda been 'ere *anexa* week."

5 A Kind of Fishing Story

or,

The Night I Lost to Jack Sharkey

I was wearing a pinstriped gray business suit the night of my memorable bout with Jack Sharkey, the former heavyweight boxing champion of the world. You don't believe it? Well, you'll believe it even less when I tell you that at the time I was running for judge.

It all happened back in the days when I still played at being a lawyer and politician—that is, before the trout had entirely captured me and taken over—and I was seeking to hold a job Governor G. Mennen "Soapy" Williams had earlier appointed me to fill when an incumbent judge had quit.

Now a candidate running for judicial office in Michigan finds himself in a bit of a bind. He can't hope to soar to victory on his party's coattails (although, for the particular job I was running for, he must first be purged of all politics by courting and winning a partisan political nomination), because of a droll state law making all judicial elections nonpartisan. He can't very well flay his opponent because that would betray lack of judicial temperament. He can't go

around making glowing promises because in court cases somebody's always got to lose. About all he can do is exude charm, try to keep his nose clean, and wish that his name was O'Brien.

After consulting the oracles I decided to concentrate my statewide campaign on Detroit. I did so for several reasons, one being that my personable young opponent hailed from there. Another was that Detroit's sylvan precincts harbored more than three times as many sterling voters as dwelt in my entire native Upper Peninsula. Yes, Detroit was clearly where the action was, so this displaced fisherman sought it and, I must say, he got it.

My campaign was slow getting off the ground. My own party dared not be nice to me, as I've said, and the other party wouldn't if it could. So it rapidly swept over me that the voters' rapture over my candidacy was remarkably containable. People stayed away from my meetings in droves, thought I did meet some pleasant janitors who had to hang around and who at least didn't throw my campaign cards away until I'd said my piece and left. There was radio and television, of course, but who wanted to contribute to the campaign fund of such a resolutely forsaken political waif?

In desperation I started haunting the auto plant gates, and to my horror discovered I'd become an invisible man. Though a towering, handsome giant in a green polka-dot tie called Soapy might occasionally penetrate their collective consciousness, the boys at the plant gates looked right through me with a sort of incurious numbness as though I wasn't there. My campaign cards dropped from their nerveless fingers faster than I could deal them out—and I'd learned dealing early at Hickey's

49

Bar. At the end of these spooky sessions I frequently went and peered in tavern mirrors to see if I was still there.

The more I campaigned the lower my spirits sagged. To add to my general depression, this was a springtime election and I was forced to miss the opening of trout season — perhaps the crowning blow. Things got so bad that only a kind of dogged loyalty and pride kept me from chucking the whole thing and fleeing north to my trout.

One night I sobbed in my beer and poured out my woes to my old friend and former college roommate Art Farrell, who worked on a Detroit newspaper. Good old redheaded Art loyally condoled with me but managed to escape before outright blubbering set in. The next morning he phoned before I was out of the sack, I having long since quit playing the role of card-dealing invisible man at the plant gate dawn patrol.

"I have a plan," Art said, and he proceeded to unfold it. Seems each spring his paper sponsored a mammoth indoor sports show, he explained, attended by throngs of sturdy citizens — and voters. One was coming up just a few days before the election and he was sure he could get me on.

"But what would I do?" I inquired glumly. "*Sing?* I'm already hoarse from shouting down the echoes of my own voice in empty halls."

"Give an exhibition of your fly-casting ability along with Jack Sharkey," Art explained. "You've already wasted most of your talents chasing trout and this could be the big vindication."

I chose to ignore Art's subtle thrust. "You mean the former heavyweight champ?" I inquired.

"Yup," Art said. "He's a boss fisherman and top fly caster now and travels all around. How about it?"

"Why not?" I said. "If I'm gonna lose the bloody election I'd sooner go down holding a fly rod than pumping the limp hands of perfect strangers."

So Art came and drove me out to the shop of my old rod-making friend Paul Young, from whom I freeloaded the loan of a balanced fly outfit for my bout, explaining to Paul that the several lovely rods I'd bought from him were naturally far away at home.

"Just think," Art mused aloud as we drove away, "you'll probably be the first opponent Jack Sharkey ever faced who's spent a whole lifetime training for a single bout."

"Planned it that way," I said, patting the slender rod case that held my secret weapon.

Came the big night and Jack and I met and shook hands in the center of the ring—I mean the casting pool —each holding his four-ounce fly rod aloft in lieu of gloves as we cagily eyed each other before the bell. Jack was a big soft-spoken guy and he chatted amiably to put me at ease while the crowd roared and the flashbulbs popped.

First Jack was introduced to the cheering multitude, and then I was. In all the din and general euphoria I quickly forgave the announcer for so mispronouncing my name that it came out sounding rather more like a brand of imported German sausage than that of any known sitting judge. Then the bell rang and we came out warily, his pinstriped Honor, I must say, feeling just a wee bit outweighed and overmatched.

First Jack, a really beautiful caster, sparred a little and threw out some conventional back casts; and then I did;

51

then, standing toe to toe, we both flailed away. Swish, swish, back and forth, away we went in a ballet of sheer rhythmic poetry. First in solo, then in duet, we finally shot the works, doing flocks of dreamy roll casts, brisk haul casts, side casts, dramatic steeple casts — the whole exciting business — while the crowd roared and roared.

Our bout ended in a delirium of applause, and I wrung Jack's big paw and he threw me a playful punch and, rallying from that, I left with my manager, Art, fairly drunk with triumph. Later, as we broke training together over at Casey's Bar, I mistily thanked my old pal Art and he solemnly assured me that *this* had been my finest hour.

"I take it all back," Art said. "I mean about wasting your time fishing."

"S'nothin' at all, pal," I said, lifting my glass. "Heresh to your health."

But the political show must grind on, and the next day, however languidly, I was back on the campaign trail. While it may have been pure illusion on my part, it somehow seemed that this time people clung to my campaign cards just a little longer before flinging them away. As the few remaining days passed I even toyed with the thought that I might win. After all, I reflected, judges had been elected for less . . .

Election Day came down to the wire and late one soft May evening I found myself in a car loaded with my staunchest supporters as they whirled me from a downtown meeting to a final one of the campaign out beyond Eight Mile Road. It was nearing midnight, we were only an hour behind schedule, and I was utterly pooped and longed to be home. As we tore along through the balmy night the thought that I'd soon be quitting this vast anonymous human hive began to obsess me.

"God, fellows," I suddenly blurted, "I wish I were up home fishing."

"Oh," my driver inquired politely, "are you a fisherman, Judgie?"

"I *love* it," I wailed, trying not to break down.

"Then you sure should have been over the Armory coupla three nights ago. Guy there could cast a fly through the eye of a needle."

"Tell me more," I said, perking up, for after all, *I*, Judgie, had been over at the Armory only a coupla three nights before.

"Never saw anything like it," another supporter put in. "Sheer poetry, that guy."

"What guy?" I inquired hopefully.

"Why ol' Jack Sharkey, of course," still another chimed in. "You know, the former heavyweight champ."

There was a considerable pause. Then: "Wasn't there some other guy there with him?" I asked in a small voice.

"Well, let's see now. Hm . . . Yeah, there *was* some character there dressed like a banker. Couldn't quite catch the name—sounded kinda Polock or Krautish. Anyway, he couldn't hold a candle to good ol' Jack."

"I wish I'd been there," I managed to croak.

The election came and went. I won. And after Art and his Ruthie and I had celebrated I raced home to go fishing, and have never been back.

6 Fly Fishermen: The World's Biggest Snobs

"Fly-fishing is such great fun," I once took a deep breath and wrote, "that it really ought to be done in bed." While I stick with this seductive notion, such an opening understandably left me little room to explore any aspects of the sport beyond certain droll romantic parallels. This was a pity because, alluring as my theory may be, there is rather more to fly-fishing than *that*.

Consequently, I've often felt a pang that I there failed to unveil still another theory I've long held about fly-fishing and the curious people it afflicts. And since the longer I fish the stronger grows my suspicion that my theory may be happening to me, I'd better get on with the unveiling while I'm still able to.

I say "able to" because to my mind—and here's my theory—fly-fishing is a progressive and hopelessly incurable disease that leaves its victims not only a little daft but high among the world's biggest snobs. At last, I've finally up and said it! (And where, ah where, is my escape passport to New Zealand?) As for my qualifications to speak, by now I am

so far over my waders in the terminal stages of the disease that I feel I've won the right to risk at least a passing comment on its pathology and some of its gaudier symptoms.

Snobbery has been defined as an insufferable affectation of superior virtue. Good as this is as far as it goes, to my mind it too much overlooks the disdainful air of condescension and outright intolerance that marks the breed. And it is here that we fly-fishermen really shine, resourcefully contriving to exhibit an unvarying intolerance toward the faults and foibles of other fishermen while remaining sublimely oblivious to our own. Fly-fishermen, in fact, have raised garden-variety snobbishness to heroic heights.

Being a crafty lot we often try to hide our true natures, occasionally going so far as to exude an air of benign indulgence toward those lost souls who fail to fish the fly. But our pose is as phony as the flies we fish, for in our hearts we regard all nonfly-fishers as meat-hunting barbarians. Why only last winter in the big corner booth at the Rainbow Bar one of our top local fly casters so far cracked up that he remarked out loud that there might be a little good in other forms of fishing. I was there and heard this astonishing heresy with my own ears.

In poor Hal's favor, I should add that we were a mixed bag of fishermen that day, including even "bait flangers," which was the way the late Tommy Cole scornfully lumped all heavers of angling hardware; Hal was caught in the benevolent glow of his third (double) bourbon; and one of the flangers present was his wife's brother—who, with the disarming guile of the breed, had already grabbed the tab.

But Hal lied, of course, and the moment the flangers left and we horrified fly-fishermen turned on him, the poor man hung his head and abjectly recanted—even to standing another round. "I was just carried away," he explained huskily, hiccuping and patting his heart. "S'matter of fack, fellas, deep down I've always known fly-fishing is to the rest of fishing what high seduction is to rape."

In his advanced stages your real-gone fly-fisherman grows critical even of his fellow fly casters, grading and calipering them as though only he held the key to some piscatorial Court of St. James's. Merely being a caster of the fly is no guarantee of admission to the sacred precincts; all *that* gets you is the right to stand in line awaiting your turn to face the inquisition.

"Is it true," a typical question might run, "that last summer you were actually seen using an automatic reel?" Should the angler confess, quick is his banishment back among the angling riffraff. A like fate awaits any poor soul ever caught using a level line, while a conviction of the major offense of using a fiber glass rod means a minimum sentence of at least five years hard labor among the girder-wielding bait casters.

Different fly-fishermen exhibit different symptoms of snobbish daffiness, of course, but my own case is sufficiently typical that I think I'll confess it as a warning to others. I was born and raised and happily still live among some of the country's most exciting and varied brown and rainbow waters. To sweeten the pot, coho and chinook salmon have lately been added.

Does lucky me daily go forth to stalk these glittering monsters? I do not. In fact I haven't even fished where

they live in several years much less impaled one. Instead
I pursue only the smaller and scarcer brook trout and
these mostly in remote back-bush ponds and beaver
dams. When ecstatic visiting anglers ask me what I think
of all the assorted piscatorial treasures all around me I
usually reply—with a snobbish sniff—that my main
reaction is one of gratitude that their well-advertised
presence has taken so much pressure off my own speckled darlings. This frequently makes them glance at one
another and shrug and sometimes even wink, a look I've
learned to interpret as meaning "How crazy can you
get?"

But visiting fishermen don't know the half of it, for my
snobbish decline is even daffier than that. Not only do I
fish solely for brook trout but, worse yet, only for *wild
native* brook trout. In fact, I'll detour miles if I hear even
a rumor that a spot I'm headed for has been planted.
One morning last summer I almost swallowed my cigar
when I caught up with a hatchery truck bouncing into
Frenchman's Pond evidently bent on a planting spree.
Both cigar and pond were spared when I learned that the
driver had merely taken a wrong turn so, forsaking all
thoughts of fishing, I got out my maps and helped speed
him out of there.

A companion quirk is the crazy leaders I use. They
must be as long and fine as I can possibly cast, so long and
dreamy in fact that I await the day when I'll get so
entwined I'll have to holler for help to get cut away. This
means a 12-foot leader for a starter, tapered to 5X,
invariably augmented by a length of 6X tippet to which,
on cloudless days, I often add a wisp of 7. On real bright
days I've longed for 8X but have so far put off using it

because it will doubtless also mean carrying a magnifying glass to tie the stuff on with. And one more gadget added to my swollen fly jacket could spell the difference between survival and drowning.

Speaking of fine leader material, I recently heard a rumor that the best of all comes from the golden tresses of Scandinavian princesses. While this sounds like a bit of a gag, so intense is the fly-fisherman's eternal search for the perfect leader that, come next winter, I'd be tempted to track the rumor down if it weren't for a companion rumor that the stuff is prohibitively expensive. This seems to be so, I gather, because genuine golden-haired princesses are not only getting harder to find but, in this age of Clairol, riskier to identify. Then too, I suppose, no matter how genuine or compliant the princess may be, once tracked down, a certain amount of hazard must accompany such a delicate royal foraging.

This brings me to a final shameful confession, one which I know I've simply got to make but have cravenly kept putting off. Maybe it would help if I led into it gently. The thing I'm driving at is this: snobbish as I know my fishing has gotten, I am aware that there are still other fishermen who've got me beat. This brings me to the brink of my confession: since it takes a snob to spot a snob, I now ruefully know I don't rate a place in the very front pew with the certified snobs. I don't for two reasons, either one of which could forever bar me from becoming a champ. One, I don't always fish a dry fly; and two, I sometimes fail to throw back all my trout.

Now I can rationalize my sins for hours on end, telling myself that it's sheer madness for any fisherman to keep forever pelting a dry fly up in this subarctic Lake Superior country, where both our seasonal and daily fly hatches tend to start late and quit early. Or again, I can repeat over and over that any guy who returns as many trout as I do—since I fish virtually every day all summer long—ought occasionally to rate keeping a few. But suave excuses get me nowhere because I know other more lionhearted fishermen who not only return all their trout but keep stoically pelting out a dry fly even on days so cold and resolutely riseless that they have to wear lined gloves to preserve a discernible pulse.

Many times I've tried to mend my ways and go straight, and sometimes I've made it for days on end. But two things usually seduce me back into sin: my corny passion for action when I go fishing and my low peasant craving for the taste of trout. After I've spent hours fishing a place I know is good and fail even to see a rise, much less get an offer at my dry, I'm apt to cave and tie on a wet or even a nymph and go slumming down where they live. Again when the pangs of hunger gnaw me, especially when I'm fishing alone, I'm often helplessly driven to creeling a few and going on a secret binge. The big thing that keeps me from becoming a genuine topflight snob is just lack of character, I guess.

Now that you've had a glimpse at the snobbish depths to which some addled fly-fishermen can descend, it sweeps over me that I still haven't come within a country mile of showing the real how and why of what makes us tick. What starts a dewy young fly-fisherman down the rocky road to snobhood? Is it all due to individual temperament or perhaps to some genetic quirk, or maybe even a constipated adolescence? Or is there something inherently snobbish in the sport itself? Anyway, ponder-

59

ing these prickly questions has made me recall a fishing incident of my youth which, if it doesn't quite explain all our queer ways, may give at least a revealing clue to how one snobbish fly-fisherman got started down his own path to perdition. If it needed a title, I think I'd call it simply "A Fly-Fisherman Is Born."

It all began over forty years ago on a lazy Sunday afternoon on the upper reaches of the lovely Jordan River in northern Lower Michigan. I had sashayed down that way from my Lake Superior bailiwick to court the girl I finally married. The poor girl should have been forewarned: on only the second day I had forsaken her to pursue the exciting new sport of fly-fishing, new to me, that is.

Though I'd been flailing away for several hours, diligently whipping up quite a froth with my spanking new fly outfit, my efforts had so far met with a remarkable lack of success. As I see it now, my failure was doubtless due to a lavish combination of two things: my own sad ineptitude plus the awesome outfit I was using.

This latter consisted of a sturdy three-piece split-bamboo fly rod for which I'd paid exactly $5.95, with postage thrown in, and which the longer I hefted the stronger became my conviction that its builder had cagily designed it to do double duty at pole vaulting. To this I had clamped an old Martin automatic reel carrying an equally venerable level silk line, both given me by one of my early fly-fishing heroes, Tommy Cole. Where I had dredged up the short bedspring coil of gut leader I was using I have mercifully forgotten, but I do recall it was strong enough to tow barges with. Upstream.

To this hawserlike leader I had tethered a giant buck-

tail streamer and, thus armed, had managed to put down every rising trout I'd so far encountered. That took a bit of doing because, back in those days, one still saw far more fish than fishermen on the lovely Jordan — not to mention those latter-day armadas of clanking canoes monotonously firing off their salvos of beer cans.

Finally, after much floundering and splashing, I made my way down to a deep partly shaded pool at the foot of a long riffle, somewhere, I believe, about Grave's Crossing. Being a little disconsolate as well as winded, I paused there to admire the view and take a five. Suddenly the mysterious calm of the pool was rudely interrupted. The biggest trout I'd seen that season exploded in its middle, sending out a series of tiny wakes. As I scrambled into position to hurl my feathered anvil, the trout again rose, and yet again.

Brandishing my rod like a knight his spear, I began whipping my huge fly back and forth, back and forth, paying out line as my gaudy harpoon screamed ever faster past my ear. Then, along with a wee prayer, I let her go and my fly plopped down into the pool with the thud of a landing capsule just as my trout rose. I struck; I missed; and I narrowly escaped losing an ear as my fly hurtled past me, successfully harpooning a lurking tree in its wild backward flight. Had I hooked the trout I have no doubt he would have landed across old Highway 66.

I had read somewhere, possibly in early Bergman, that canny fly-fishermen always rested a startled trout, so I splashed out of there and toiled up the steep bank and retrieved my fly from an overhanging elm. Then I composed myself under its shade to watch the pool. After ten minutes of craftily resting my prize, with still no rise, I

debated getting the hell out of there and maybe at least
raising a beer.

"Maybe I stunned him," I mused, perhaps not entirely
an outside speculation considering the fly I was using.
Finally I decided to give him another ten minutes, so I lit
a cigar and pored over my lone fly box, admiring my
dozen or so equally imposing flies, all decorated in various colors, all the time waiting for my trout to become
unstartled.

Two low-flying ducks came hurtling upstream just as
my giant trout rose. For a second I had a wild thought
he'd risen for them, but no, they were wheeling round
the upstream bend as he rose once again. So again I got
out my fly box with trembling hands and pored over
my feathered treasures, finally choosing and tying on
another giant streamer of equal caliber and fire power
but rather different hue. I had already learned, you see,
that we crafty fly-fishermen had to vary our subtle offerings.

I glanced downstream to plan the angle of my new
assault and my heart sank. Another fisherman was
wading round the downstream bend, fishing as he came,
headed straight for my private pool. As I sat watching
him inch along, listening to the slow rhythmic whish of
his casts, my feeling of resentment at his presence turned
gradually to admiration and then to concern—admiration for his superb casting ability; concern lest at any
moment he be swept away.

For as he drew closer I saw that my intruder was a very
old man, incredibly fragile and spindly, looking as
though he'd be far more at home in a wheelchair attended by a nurse than out here alone breasting a power-

63

ful stream. He was in water up to the limit of his waders, precariously teetering and balancing, pluckily bucking the current with a tall wading staff. As I watched with growing apprehension, the macabre thought flashed over me that if he sneezed about then he'd surely ship water and that if *I* sneezed he might even drown.

But on he came, slowly, coolly, apparently serenely unruffled by the glorious trout rising steadily between us. It was the only riser in sight, in fact, but still the old man did not hurry, fishing every inch of the riseless water between himself and the pool, delivering each loving cast as though it were his very last.

I leaned forward tensely when the old man had worked himself into casting range for *our* trout. But no, he still was not ready; instead, with cupped hand he was lunging at the surface, seeking (I sagely concluded with an assist from Bergman) a specimen of the floating naturals. Finally he caught one, which he studied at length through a little glass. Then, still using his glass, he began producing and poring over a series of fly boxes that could have stocked both Abercrombie's and Mills and Son. Then he found and pounced on his prize like a dieting dowager plunging for a bonbon. Then came the slow tying on of his new fly, then the hand testing of fly against leader. When finally he straightened and faced our steadily feeding trout, I sighed and weakly sat back.

"Wheesh!" went his line as he deftly fed it out in short side casts, gradually lengthening it and facing more upstream, the line now undulating like a fleeing serpent, even to a low screaming hiss. Back and forth it went, drawing ever closer, ever back and forth, lazily back and forth, in a kind of surrealist ballet.

Then came a forward cast during which he seemed subtly to stiffen and brace himself; then the sudden release, with both arms held high like a diver's, and I marveled as the line coiled forward like a lash high above the pool, seeming to hang poised for a moment before ever so gently descending, the leader dreamily curling forward like the unfolding of a ballerina's arm, the tiny fly itself settling last upon the water with the languid grace of a wisp of airborne thistledown.

The fly circled uncertainly for a moment and barely began its brave descent when the trout rose and engulfed it in one savage roll. The old man flicked his skinny wrist to set the hook and the battle was on. All the while I sat there tensely watching, hypnotized, drinking in the memorable scene, watching an old man's skill pitted against this dripping eruption of nature, watching the gallant trout's frantic rushes and explosions followed by periods of sulking calm as it bored deep, trying to escape its barbed tormentor, the throbbing line and leader vibrating like the plucked string of a harp, watching even the firefly winking as a succession of tiny spray-born rainbows magically came and went.

I do not know how long it was before the old man had lowered his net into the water and, almost before I knew it, was straining and holding aloft a glistening, dripping, German brown trout of simply enormous proportions. Again I watched closely as the old man turned his sagging net this way and that, admiring his catch, nodding at it, seeming even to be whispering to it, then carefully unhooking it and—here I almost fell off my perch— with both hands gently lowering his prize to the water where, with a sudden flash, it took off and away.

65

"Bravo!" I leapt to my feet and shouted, thrilled and carried away by the superb performance I had just witnessed.

I had startled the old man and he did a quick little balancing act during which he doubtless shipped some water because, as he peered up at me testily over his glasses, he emitted a grunting sound and, scowling, looked away.

"Look, Mister," I shouted, emboldened by this warm show of fishing camaraderie, "wouldn't it be much safer and easier if you turned around and fished downstream?"

This time I'd really shaken him; it was as though I'd struck him with a stone. Again the quick little jig from which he soon rallied to give me a withering glance, peering up at me as though studying some species of gnat, all the while making funny noises in his throat. Then it came.

"Young fellow," he quavered in a high falsetto voice fairly dripping with scorn, "I'd sooner be over on the Ironton ferry dock settin' on my ass plunkin' for bass than ever fish a wet fly downstream!"

"Yessir," I said, hanging my head, sneaking out of there with burning ears, making a wide detour downstream and then stealthily back to the river, where, from behind a protective clump of bushes I secretly watched the old man at his devotionals.

And as I watched and mused I was overtaken by a vision, and presently found myself dreaming a wistful dream that someday, some way, I would be able to fish and carry on like this magnificent old goat.

7 Size Is Not the Measure

The other day I ran across a fishing article in a Detroit newspaper that filled me with delight and melancholy. The part that particularly caught me was a reference to a recent claim made by a state fish biologist that, in his opinion, more and more fishermen were turning away from the pursuit of brook trout in favor of other species of trout and salmon, particularly the generally larger- and faster-growing brown.

My delight came from learning of the lessening of competition for what still remains *my* favorite fish, all state fish biologists to the contrary, the lovely brook trout; my melancholy over the realization that evidently our national passion for bigness for bigness' sake was now afflicting even my fellow fishermen.

The article went on to say—and I took no joy at all from this—that this growing obsession with bigger fish was already affecting many state planting programs and that, in response to mounting clamor for vaster piscatorial targets to pelt away at, fewer and fewer brook trout were being

planted compared with burlier specimens.

Pondering this sad news it suddenly swept over me that, come to think of it, I hadn't seen a single picture of a brook trout adorning any of the outdoor magazines in many months—or was it years? Their places had instead been taken by gaping specimens of heavyweight trout or salmon — not to mention a growing variety of deep-sea monsters—being held aloft at risk of hernia by smirking fishermen who could often be distinguished from their victims only by their grins.

The more I brooded over this sad state of affairs the more my melancholy deepened, and it did so for a variety of reasons. First of all I felt that this new obsession with bigger and bigger fish was inevitably transplanting to our trout waters the whole competitive, strident, screechingly acquisitive world of business. Worse yet, that in doing so, fishermen were sacrificing one of the main rewards and solaces of going fishing at all, namely, that fishing is—or at least used to be—the world's only sport that's fun even to fail at. Further, by making an ego massage out of this ancient sport, these deluded souls were actually creating more not less frustrated and unhappy fishermen for the simple reason that the more fishermen there were who panted only after big fish naturally the fewer big fish there would be left to be caught. Finally it struck me as sad beyond words that fishermen themselves would let one of the world's oldest and loveliest contemplative pastimes turn into a competitive rat race much as we have allowed modern basketball to degenerate into sort of a commercialized polka played only by bored pituitary freaks.

All of which brings me to one of my own big-fish

experiences. It all happened back in the distant days when you could still buy a decent split-bamboo fly rod for under thirty bucks. Hank and I had been fishing what I shall call Big River — for that was not its name — all that hot sunny Sunday with little luck. Toward late afternoon, bouncing out in the Model A, we decided to take a quick look at a certain slow deep bend at the foot of a long run of white water.

Nothing but juniors were rising, and we were about to resignedly take off when Hank spotted some splashy risers a little way upstream, above the fast water. Immediately he began twitching and champing to have after them. Would I care to join him? he magnanimously inquired, his voice suddenly grown hoarse with excitement.

"You go, pal," I swiftly said, waving him away with the back of my hand, the soul of generosity. "Anyway you spotted 'em first and moreover I'm hungry and pooped, not to mention still a little hung over, so I'll just stay down here and see what happens."

"Don't catch 'em all," Hank said, eagerly splashing away upstream.

Half an hour later Hank had disappeared around a distant upstream bend. Meanwhile I had caught and released at least a half-dozen juvenile brookies. Dusk started falling, along with my spirits, so I sighed and plumped myself down on the damp bank and lit an Italian cigar and swatted away at mosquitoes and wondered what in hell I was doing there. Swirling bats soon joined the swarms of mosquitoes and, far overhead, I could occasionally hear the soaring screech and the diving *spung* of hunting nighthawks.

69

A fish rose above me, scarcely ten feet away and virtually inshore. Another junior leaguer, I thought, and I sat there idly debating whether I should bother to get up and try for it, my drowned little Adams trailing idly in the water below me. The fish rose again, making a neat little dimple and, still sitting, I executed a lazy-man's side-wheeling roll cast, flipping my sodden fly upstream where it landed in the fading circle with a genteel plop.

The fish took it underwater, ever so gently, and I flipped my wrist to set the fly and then jerked my rod to bring the foolish juvenile closer so I could release him. Nothing budged, and instead my line and leader grew taut and my rod bowed into a daisy hoop.

"Damn," I said aloud, "the little devil's got me snagged," and I wearily got to my feet to go unsnag myself.

With my first splashing step upstream my "snag" started moving out into deeper water. Curious and still unbelieving, I cautiously pumped the fish up to the surface for a look and almost swallowed my cigar when I beheld a dark dorsal fin cleaving the water at least a foot back from the end of my throbbing leader. I took another step, the fish made a powerful rush for deep water, and the battle was on.

At least an hour later Hank came splashing downstream and played his flashlight on a huddled figure still clenching a cold cigar in his teeth, his bone-tired wrist still glued to his straining daisy hoop.

"What in hell *is* it?" Hank asked in an awed voice.

70

"Dunno, Hank," I answered weakly, "but it sure feels like an overweight mermaid."

"Let's take a look," Hank said, holding his flash close to

the dark water. We both gasped when we saw the proportions of the monster brown I was on to, its gills now gulping uncertainly, the great fish half-lying on its side. Ten minutes later I drew the fatigued creature inshore and, using both arms as a scoop—my landing net wouldn't begin to take him—somehow tossed him up on the bank and fell beside him where we both lay for a long time, panting and exhausted.

This is the second most memorable fish I ever caught. It is memorable not only because I have never before or since played any fish for nearly so long but also because I caught him on a Size 16 Adams tied onto a 5X tapered nylon leader testing to barely two pounds. How I ever held on to him I still do not quite know, but I suspect it was a lucky combination of the dreamy relaxation of a hangover plus the curious fact that this big fish foolishly failed to try to leave the pool while still fresh enough to have easily cleaned me out.

Since then I have caught several bigger rainbows and coho salmon, though how much bigger I cannot say because in all the excitement of that distant Sunday I clean forgot to weigh and measure my memorable brown. Yet this gallant brown remains memorable not because of his size but mainly because of the improbable tackle I took him on.

Today there is scarcely an outdoor magazine or fishing whatnot that doesn't regularly display small regiments of anglers proudly displaying even more "monstorious" fish than my memorable brown. Most of these pictures leave me cold for one simple reason: they rarely reveal the size and strength of the tackle they were taken on. Lacking that crucial information it strikes me this whole

71

repetitious big-fish picture gallery is nothing more than a dreary and boring parade of champion winchers and weight lifters.

If catching this monster brown was my second most memorable fishing experience, how much bigger, one may ask, was my most memorable fish? The answer is he wasn't nearly so large, and in fact my big brown could probably have devoured him in a single gulp, sans salt or pepper. For the really memorable thing is that I took this fourteen-inch brookie last year on Frenchman's Pond (don't look for it on any map) on a Size 20 Jassid, hooking him over a tangled underwater logjam and somehow dancing him out of there and finally landing him, using a basic 5X leader with a 7X tippet testing to barely a pound. The feat was so memorable, in fact, that I finally released the tired fish as a reward for gallantry.

Any fisherman who feels proud over catching a monster fish (or indeed any game fish) on a hawser is just as deluded, it strikes me—and should feel just as ashamed —as those virile chest-thumping hunters who continue to bombard our fragile native antelopes with elephant guns. It isn't the *quantity* of the fish caught that counts; its the *quality* of the means used in catching him. To paraphrase the old jazz song, it ain't what you catch but the way that you catch it.

My old nonfishing lawyer friend, Parnell McCarthy, recently put his finger on it. We were enshrined in the Rainbow Bar having a late-afternoon quiet one together and the old boy was idly fingering a fishing catalog I'd just gotten in the day's mail.

"All a bunch of craptitude," he said, flashing me a picture of a regiment of grinning fishermen displaying

73

their assorted Loch Lomond monsters. "The trouble with these damn fish pictures is they fail to furnish identification charts telling who caught whom." He wagged his head. "You fishing guys are getting as obsessed with size as the judges of our so-called beauty contests."

"What do you mean?" I inquired politely.

"Any aspiring beauty queen may have the face of a madonna, the soul of a swooping angel, the mind of an Einstein," he sang out like an auctioneer, holding his empty glass aloft, "but if she don't possess a pair of bustolas at least size 36 she ain't never gonna git picked queen of nothin'." He banged his glass on our table. "They're not beauty but booby contests."

"Amen," I said, banging my own glass. "You can repeat that again."

"Coming up!" Polly the ever-alert proprietor hollered from behind the bar.

8 D. McGinnis: Guide

Old bald-pated droopy-mustached Danny McGinnis and his "boys"—four aging bachelors who, though all younger than Dan, were either pressing or had already overtaken their sixties—lived in an old log bunkhouse abandoned by logger Andy Ferguson around the turn of the century. This rambling old structure had been christened Andy's Fleabag by the realistic lumberjacks who'd slept in it, but during the Depression Danny and the boys had changed its name to the equally realistic one of Hungry Hollow, and that it had remained.

Hungry Hollow stood on the extreme westerly rim of the Mulligan Plains where they sheer off into the valley of the Big Dead River. These broad plains had once been covered by a vast stand of virgin white pine, but all that logger Andy Ferguson had left behind, besides one bug-ridden bunkhouse, was miles of charred and weathered stumps looking like tombstones in some abandoned cemetery, although some occasional passing fishermen felt they rather more resembled bleak accusing monuments to man's

relentless war on nature.

The only regular work Danny and his boys ever did was to try to figure out new ways to avoid doing any regular work. This sometimes proved exhausting but had for the most part always paid off because the boys pretty much lived off the land — hunting, fishing, trapping, or hopefully foraging for overlooked vegetables in their rabbit-haunted garden plot—plus pooling their several assorted pensions and social security checks and Timmy's disabled veteran payments into a common treasury jealously presided over by old Danny himself.

Trout naturally formed an important staple of the diet of the boys of Hungry Hollow because, after all, the lovely Big Dead River made an obliging U-shaped bend just below their door. And when the fishing palled, Danny and the boys could sit outside for hours on a summer evening just swapping stories and swatting mosquitoes and watching the feeding trout rising in the river below.

"Lookit dem yiggers yumping," Swan would sometimes say, pointing. "Eff Ay din't know no better Ay vould svear it vere raining hail."

But tonight no trout were rising on the Big Dead River below Hungry Hollow. They weren't because it was still not yet the end of March and snow still lingered in the valley and the river was still clogged with chunks of floating ice. Moreover, aside from the gloomy weather, a general aura of gloom pervaded the Hollow, largely because the camp treasury was not only flat broke but two of the boys were in jail—casualties of the boys' annual Saint Patrick's Day trek to the town of Chippewa. True, all such annual treks tended to verge on calamity, but this particular Saint Patrick's Day excursion had approached outright disaster.

First Big Buller Beaudin had resented some ill-timed barroom remarks concerning the genesis and possible contents of his enormous belly, and when the smoke cleared away the place had been left strewn with broken glass and inert townsmen. Then Buller had piled up the camp Model A trying to escape the cops, thus leaving the boys without transportation. Finally, old Danny had to empty the waning camp treasury paying all the assorted fines and doctor's bills needed to keep Buller out of jail.

As if this weren't bad enough, Swan and Taconite had gone on a little spree of their own and gotten picked up for drunk and disorderly and, the camp treasury now being depleted, had each drawn and were serving thirty days in jail. Only nondrinking Timmy and old Danny had escaped the clutches of the law, but Timmy had added to the camp's woes by buying and charging an expensive new fly rod he said he just simply had to have. Yes, Hungry Hollow was in a bad way: too early for fishing, no car to ride to town in, two of the boys still in jail, and the treasury not only empty but deep in debt.

So on this raw late March night as the wind grieved in the camp chimney, old Danny glumly presided over a post-Saint Patrick's Day wake. Poor Swan and Taconite were still in jail, of course. Buller sat darning his favorite sweater—the principal casualty of his barroom brawl— his moist rosebud lips working in rhythm with each darn, while slender Timmy, the camp's reigning intellectual, sat at the oilclothed table reading a dog-eared copy of *American Sportsman*. And all the while a parched and boozeless Danny, treasurer of Hungry Hollow's busted

77

treasury, was reduced to bottling his latest batch of home-brewed beer.

Whether or not it is true that every cloud has a silver lining, as the old song says, it was at this magic moment that the great solution was born. Timmy looked up from his reading, blinking thoughtfully, and glanced over at Danny, whose cheeks were sunken like those of a victim of pellagra as he strove to start siphoning off a new crock.

"I see by an ad here, Dan," Timmy said quietly, "where some fellas down in Wisconsin is askin' twelve bucks a day for boardin' and guidin' *bass* fishermen—with boat rent extra." Timmy paused and shook his head over the wonder of it all. "Just imagine," he snorted, "payin' all that dough just to fish them lousy crummy bass! An' here we got a lovely river right outside our door fairly crawlin' with beautiful rainbows and browns." Timmy shook his head and daintily moistened his finger to turn the page.

Danny still had the siphon hose in his mouth, his cheeks bulging with raw new beer, and he frantically wigwagged Timmy not to turn the page. "*Pah!*" he finally exclaimed, extracting and pinching the hose and at the same time spewing a stream of bitter new beer across the room. Buller must have got caught in some of the spray because he quickly looked up from his darning and held his needle poised in midair, wistfully moistening his lips.

"Look!" Danny exclaimed, "lemme see that there ad!" As Timmy handed him the magazine and Danny adjusted his ten-cent-store glasses and read it, his voice grew hoarse with excitement. "Look, Timmy, Buller—if

them Wisconsin birds can git sech big dough fer lettin'
city dudes ketch them slobby tourist bass, why can't *we* do
the same thing fer lettin' 'em fish the lovely beauties
down in our river below?"

"You mean—?" Timmy began, enlightenment dawning.

"Zackly," Danny said. "Get out your paper and pencil,
me lad."

While a gradually nodding Buller alternately darned
and dozed, still in the grip of his Saint Patrick's Day
celebration, Danny and Timmy worked far into the night
on their new ad aimed at making Hungry Hollow a
mecca for jaded city fishermen. Naturally they'd run
their first ad in a Chicago newspaper, because naturally
every small town in America has its "big town" and
Chicago happened to be Chippewa's.

"How much'll we charge 'em?" Timmy asked the camp
treasurer, holding his pencil poised.

"Hm, le's see now," Danny said, sipping his mustache
and working his bushy eyebrows and rubbing his bald
head. "Of course they's naturally gonna have to pay
more gittin' way up here past them Wisconsin bass pud-
dles. Le's see — maybe we should ought to charge 'em
half price, like say six bucks a head for found an' lodgin'
— with guide service thrun in."

"Six bucks it is," Timmy said, filling in the missing item
and presenting the finished ad to Danny with a nice
secretarial flourish. Danny again adjusted his glasses
and, his voice cracked with emotion, read it aloud to
Timmy by the wavering lamplight, Buller having long
since crept off to bed.

NOTICE

I got brown trout and rainbows up here at Hungry Hollow big as Eskimo dogs. You capture 'em and I'll cook 'em. Rate $6 per head per day for food and lodging—with free expert guide service thrun in. Write me c/o Polly's Rainbow Bar, Chippewa, Mich.

Resp.
D. McGinnis, guide

"Boy," Danny rapturously breathed, rubbing the mist out of his eyes, "that there's so purty I'm all kinda swole up inside." He shook his head. "Timmy, you're a goddam genius an' your ad is pure American litterchewer."

Timmy's contribution to American literature worked like a charm; the first reservations came by airmail within three days of the appearance of the ad. "Will arrive on the midnight train from Chicago on May first," Dr. Sawyer's letter ran. "My three fishing pals and I plan to spend the balance of that night at your local hotel. Please await us there."

The wounded camp Model A still remained in Chippewa unrepaired, so about midafternoon on the first day of May Danny bade the boys good-bye and took off on the long hike to town to meet the first batch of city fishermen. Swan and Taconite had by now served their time and were out of jail and so a farewell delegation of all four of the boys lined up to wave him off. Luck was with Danny—or was it?—for about halfway to town he caught a ride on a logging truck and arrived in Chippewa still long before dark not only with time on his hands but a consuming thirst in his throat.

Danny would have preferred to wait in the informal atmosphere of the Rainbow Bar or indeed almost any-place other than the fancy new Cliff Dwellers Inn where the town swells and mining crowd hung out. But Dr. Sawyer's letter had been pretty plain on that point, hadn't it, that Danny should head for the Inn? Danny reread the letter and, yes, there was no mistake. But wait! The letter didn't say *where* in the Inn he had to wait, so Danny, who always had a keen instinct for the best place to wait, smiled and headed for the street entrance to the Inn's Colonial Taproom.

The place was crowded with laggard devotees of the cocktail hour and Danny, making his first visit there and unaccustomed to the subdued lights, groped his way to an empty stool up at the bar. The dapper young bar-tender, fresh out of Duluth, eyed Danny up and down, from his old round undented felt hat, his aromatic plaid hunting jumper, his floppy woolen high-water stag pants, to his incredibly muddy high-top boots.

"May I be of help to you, sir?" he said with practiced disdain.

"You sure in hell kin, young fella," Danny shot back, his mustaches bristling, "an' I'd like to compliment you fer readin' my mind."

"Yes?" the young bartender said with infinite patience. "What will it be, sir?"

"I'll take a double shot of pile-run whiskey," Danny all but roared, throwing his jackknife and a pile of loose change down on the bar.

81

"And what would you prefer for a mix, sir?"

"Whaddya mean mix?" Danny barked, totally at sea before such esoteric barroom palaver.

"Whaddya want for a wash?" the young bartender grated, finally lapsing into the more familiar idiom of those chronic connoisseurs of pile-run whiskey.

"*Gin!*" Danny shot back, whereupon the barroom patrons giggled and roared and tossed down their dry martinis while the skimpily-gowned lady at the piano quickly struck up a tune and old Danny tossed off his drink and ordered still another double round. Spring was in the air . . .

The midnight train from Chicago duly arrived and disgorged the four Chicago fishermen and their mounds of duffel and fishing gear. The fishermen proceeded to the Cliff Dwellers Inn and searched high and low for their missing host and guide—but Danny was nowhere to be found. Finally, smelling a rat, they sensibly made their way down to the Colonial Taproom from where, putting several clues together, they extended their search out the side-street door adjoining the hotel's imposing new rock garden. There they were met by the strange midnight tableau of the Inn's little Cornish gardener trying to dislodge a snoring interloper from his pet new flower beds.

"Damme, man, you're a-lyin' all hover me crocus 'n' tulip beds, that you are!" Cooky was shouting, all the while tugging away at and trying to arouse the inert guide of the unmet Chicago fishermen. "Come aout of there, Mister Danny, you hintoxicated bum."

"Just a moment, we'll give you a hand," Dr. Sawyer said, and so the four Chicago fishermen dug Danny out of Cooky's flower beds and reverently carried him off upstairs for transplanting in a different bed.

"'E 'urted my flawers, 'e 'urted my flawers," little Cooky wailed as the procession filed away, doing a skinny dance of anger at midnight in the spring.

Danny had survived and rallied from worse adventures than an evening spent mixing whiskey with gin and sleeping in dampish rock gardens, so the next morning he was almost his old chipper self again after he had polished off a lumberjack breakfast in the hotel dining room. Feeling his responsibilities he later guided his guests over to Burke's livery stable and helped haggle over the price of the car and trailer they rented to haul themselves and their gear up to Hungry Hollow.

"How do you feel now, Mr. McGinnis?" inquired Raymond, the driver and one of the Chicago fishermen, as their cavalcade thundered across the loose planking of the bridge over Barnhardt Creek.

"Who, me?" Danny said, starting out of a little nap. "I feel like havin' another drink."

"Before *noon*?" Raymond said, aghast.

"Why not, why not?" Danny said, winking and spreading his hands. "After all, the only time I'll ever *take* a drink is during and between meals. Strickly temperance, that's me."

Dr. Sawyer sighed and produced and passed back a bottle of city whiskey upon which Danny played a long unbroken solo, deftly drying his mustaches on his jumper sleeve when he was done. "You boys havin' a little snort, too?" he finally said, remembering his manners, making as though to surrender the bottle.

83

"Heavens no," Dr. Sawyer said, as the others recoiled and swiftly shook their heads. "We came way up here to catch some of those gorgeous trout you described in that intriguing ad of yours. We're in training for that, see? Fishing before drinking, see?"

"You've a point there," Danny conceded after judiciously pondering. "Jest thought you might, lads. Now me, I'm used to drinkin' before fishin' 'cause our water's so fearful cold a man needs a touch to steady his castin' arm. 'Smatter of fack it gives me a little chill even thinkin' of it. Mind if I have a wee drop more?"

"Go 'head, Dan," Dr. Sawyer said, shrugging and finally surrendering. "But it would be real nice, you being our guide and all, if you'd sort of manage to stay sober enough just long enough to kind of point out the river to us."

But Danny's bald head had already sagged down on his chest in lip-puttering slumber, from which he did not rouse until they rumbled across the bridge over Mulligan Creek.

"Almost there, boys," he chirped brightly as the rented car and trailer labored up the long sandy hill to the top of the treeless Mulligan Plains. "Take the first fork to the left fer Hungry Hollow."

"What's that water I see gleaming between those tall evergreen trees down beyond that tarpaper shack?" Dr. Sawyer suddenly asked, pointing.

"That there's the Big Dead River where you guys is gonna fish," their guide explained, adding after a pause, "An' that tarpaper shack you jest mentioned happens to be Hungry Hollow where I lives. It's also the place you boys'll be stayin'—that's unless you prefer comootin' back and forth between here an' that fancy Inn. Jest say the word, boys — "

"Oh no, no, no," Dr. Sawyer apologized, swiftly passing back the city bottle to heal the sudden breach.

"Wups, watch out fer my truck garden, young fella," Danny called out after the breach was magnificently healed. "Better park over next to the outhouse there an' have everythin' handy."

"And who are those four guys standing out in front?" Doc shrilled.

"Oh, them's jest four ol' pals who happen' to drop by one by one durin' Depression days an' who been stayin' on temporary ever since. Jest here on a li'l visit."

"But Danny, the Depression was years and *years* ago, man!"

"By God, so it was," Danny agreed. "How the bloody time flies. My, my . . . Well here we are, boys—welcome to Hungry Hollow." He held up his cupped hand and beckoned his waiting boys with five gnarled and knotty fingers. "C'mon over here, boys, an' I'll take an' interdoosh you."

2

After a quick lunch that featured Swan's fresh home-baked bread, the city fishermen pawed away at their mounds of luggage and gradually crawled into their uniforms. It was decided that all four would start fishing from the big pool below camp, flipping coins to decide which two would start fishing upstream and which other pair down. So prolonged were their preparations, in fact, that Danny was able to spear several quick drinks from the waning bottle. When at length the four were armed and ready, Carl, one of the city fishermen, asked Danny if he planned to join them fishing.

"Mebbe later, not right now," Danny said, squinting up at the sun from his seat on the camp sawbuck. "Little too bright. Anyway, ol' Danny's only the goddam guide—an' at Hungry Hollow the golden rule is 'payin' gents first.' "

"But where's your rod, your waders, and all your gear?" Raymond asked.

"No problem," Danny said, walking over to the side of the camp and taking down a battered set-up bamboo fly rod resting on two rusty nails. Each joint was held together by adhesive tape, the cracked level line tied to a coiled piece of bedspring leader to which in turn was attached a massive hair fly adorning a hook that seemed big enough to fasten screen doors.

"Won the hull outfit in a firemen's tournament raffle in Chippewa sixteen — no, seventeen years ago," Danny explained, patting his pet.

"But your waders — your net and creel and all?"

"Don't use none," Danny said, rolling his eyes. "Saves all kinds of money fer charities an' to give them missionary fellas fer convertin' heathens with."

The Chicago fishermen averted their eyes, glancing at each other with expressions that eloquently said "what have we gotten into?"

Led by old Danny, their expert guide, they slithered and slipped their way down the steep trail to the starting Big Dead pool.

"That's it," Danny said, pointing, and the four city fishermen stood gazing at the vast pool churning restlessly in the sun, hissing and boiling like some giant

witch's cauldron. "Might so well give it a try here. Same price." He then leaned his ancient rod against a tree and climbed uphill and sat on a sun-warmed rock safely out of casting range.

Raymond was the first to select and tie on the maiden fly — a downy small dry — expertly placing a graceful thistle cast into the very center of the pool. There was a sudden silvery flash and the line grew taut for an instant and then went limp.

"Whoopee!" shouted Raymond, doing a clumsy little bewadered jig. "Cleaned out on my first cast! *Whoopee!*"

"Hm," Danny said, half to himself, sitting up on his sunny perch. "Mebbe they'll be on the prod after all." He then busied himself taking on and working up a new chew of tobacco while the Chicago fishermen got under way. Two of them took and returned fairish brook trout on their first pool casts — "Small fry," Danny said — and he still sat watching as each twosome disappeared around their respective bends. Meanwhile no more big fish struck.

Once alone, Danny rose and spat and reached in his jumper and pulled out a fresh bottle of Chicago whiskey he'd somehow stumbled across and played a solo in the sun. He then descended to the water, grabbed his rod, and sat soaking his leader in the pool, stripping out line, waiting for a passing cloud to come obscure the sun.

"Ah," he breathed as the sun finally left the pool, and he reached in his jumper and pulled out a slice of Swan's freshly baked bread. Breaking off and wadding a small piece, he tossed it out into the pool. There was a quick silvery flash and the bread disappeared. He then reached for his rod and casually flipped his fly where the fish had risen.

"*Clap!*" went the striking fish, and Danny struck back, and lo he was on to a real beauty. He dropped his rod and grabbed the line, calmly pulling in the threshing fish, hand over hand, deftly unhooking the fish and dropping it into the game bag of his jumper. Once again he cast his bread upon the waters and again not in vain. Before the sun emerged he had caught two rainbows and a brown, each running well over two pounds.

"Guess mebbe the big ones ain't here today," Danny remarked to himself. "Yep, yep — guess mebbe I'll have me another snort an' meander downstream."

Meanwhile, Dr. Sawyer and Thaddeus worked their way slowly downstream, fishing with the easy precision and grace of finished experts. After all, they'd waited all winter for this golden moment, and here they were fishing virtually virgin water except for the alcoholic flounderings of one old man armed with a primitive fly rod one might better beat rugs with.

The firm graveled bottom, rarely over waist deep, made ideal wading, and the air sang with the sylvan whine and whish of their lovely casts. Not a single pocket or ripple did they miss. Once Thaddeus got a boiling rise from a really big one, but missed the strike. Both took several decent brook trout, and a few juniors, all of which they carefully returned, for *they* were after the big ones. But so far the big ones were not after them . . .

Perhaps a mile below the starting pool Doc and Thaddeus paused and held a strategy council. Could it be that old Danny was right and that it was far too bright for good fishing?

"Except for Raymond's clean-out up at the pool and the one I missed," Thaddeus said, a little despondently, "I'd swear there weren't any big trout in this river."

89

"Let's work our way back upstream," Doc said, recalling the lovely starting pool. "Maybe old Danny can suggest another stretch."

"I'd guess our guzzling old guide is safely up in bed by now," Thaddeus said, standing on a gravel bar and playing in a seven-inch brook trout.

"That's if he's sober enough to climb the hill," Doc said, pausing on the same gravel bar and changing to another fly. "I wonder what the old goat's up to?"

Their answer came abruptly as they heard a prolonged *"Haloo-oo-oo"* and then beheld Danny rounding the upstream bend, splashing and floundering in the middle of the river, his venerable fly rod bent double before him like a graduation hoop.

"Haloo-oo," he called again, and it was then that the enchanted city fishermen saw that old Danny was being towed, hauled, and tugged downstream by the grandfather of all giant trout, the snout of which occasionally showed above the water several rod lengths ahead of Dan.

"Loo'gout!" Danny shrilled, his skinny shanks working like pistons. "Here I come — clear the goddam way!"

But the two transfixed Chicago fishermen could only stand gaping on their gravel bar as old Danny and his fish swiftly descended upon them.

"Spung!" went Danny's leader as it snapped and broke just as the giant fish, in the blind fury of its run, charged clear up onto the gravel bar and lay flopping and panting at the Chicago fishermen's feet.

"Grab 'im!" Danny cackled in cold horror, but by now the hypnotized fishermen were beyond all movement. Then, just as the giant fish made a final riverward flop, Danny sailed through the air in a superb flying tackle

90

and landed on top of Grampaw —*whoosh!*—where both of them lay for a long time very wet and very still.

It took three drinks from Doc's emergency flask to bring old Danny around. "Who hit me?" Danny demanded, sitting up slowly and holding his side. "Who'd hit a pore sickly ol' man?"

The game bag of his jumper had come open, strewing lovely rainbow and brown trout everywhere.

"Oo me pore side," Danny said, clutching at his left rib cage. "Oo, gimme 'nother swaller of that there booze— can't even breathe withouten 'nother swaller."

Dr. Sawyer carefully fed Danny another drink and then opened his jumper and shirt and felt his left side, Danny all the while wincing and squirming.

"Do you think I'm a little pregnant, Doc?" Danny asked when Doc was done.

"No," Doc said after pondering a bit, "but I'd guess, lacking X rays, that landing your big rainbow has cost you between three and four cracked ribs on your left side."

"'Tis well worth it," Danny said, gingerly reaching over and patting his big fish and then vainly trying to stagger to his feet. "Why don't you boys fetch the fish and we'll go back to camp where Swan'll cook 'em up and we'll all sorta celebrate like? What d'you say, boys?"

Doc and Thaddeus looked at each other and silently nodded and gathered up Danny and all the fish and splashed away upstream in the dappled sunlight. Old Danny, full of visions of the frolic ahead, even managed to break into a quavering song, one of his favorite ditties:

91

> *Oh when I'm dead an' in me grave,*
> *An' no more whiskey will I crave,*

On my tombstone let this be wrote,
'Ten thousand quarts run down his throat!'

3

The next morning the Chicago fishermen awoke
throbbing of pulse and coated of tongue and groped
their way to the water pail in the best Hungry Hollow
tradition. But old Danny soon had them relaxed and
smiling with a couple rounds of Highland Flings, a po-
tent drink of guaranteed therapy, the secret of which
Danny carefully explained.

"Jest take a tripler of Hungry Hollow moonshine, a
dash of lemon juice, a little sugar, and add some boiling
water," he explained, holding up a warning finger. "But
mind, you dassen't put too much water. Yep, yep, never
too much water."

After breakfast he presented his guests with some of
Timmy's big home-tied bucktail flies—"Big flies fer big
fish," he explained—and lectured them for ten minutes
on the need for caution and patience in stalking the big
ones. "Come, lads, get your gear an' let me show you."

Walking like an aging Junker general in his rigid new
corset of adhesive tape, Danny led his guests down to the
pool and initiated them into the ritual of casting one's
bread upon the water.

"Git ready, now, one of you," he said, tossing out a
wadded morsel of bread, and —*bang*— a grinning Dr.
Sawyer was soon fast to a tail-standing dandy.

"Good luck, boys," Danny said, leaving them there still
watching Doc fighting his fish. "Pea soup's on the menoo
tonight an' I gotta go help Swan get that started."

The Chicago fishermen had a great day and each caught and returned several lovely browns and rainbows — but none in the same league as Grampaw, of course. That night at supper they were exultant and clamored for another celebration. The next morning they even beat Danny up clamoring for their Highland Flings. And so the days dreamily slipped by.

They overstayed their leave by three days and when they left presented Danny with a brand-new fly rod and reel and double-tapered line. They also insisted upon paying double for their keep. Moreover they made solemn reservations to return the following May. "Daniel," Dr. Sawyer concluded, "we've never seen anything to match either this superb place or your excellent canny guiding."

"Thanks," Danny said, busily putting together his handsome new fly rod.

"Good-bye, Danny," they called out, waving, as they pulled away. "See you next May if not sooner."

"Yep, yep," Danny said from the camp doorway, saluting them briefly with two crooked fingers.

Buller and the boys, who'd been off cutting firewood up near Connors Creek, rushed into camp an hour later to conduct the audit. There they found an absorbed and bespectacled Danny sitting at the oilcloth table counting out greenbacks into neat little piles.

"Le's see," he was saying, "four gents fer eight days at twelve bucks a head makes — hm — what the hell *does* it make?"

"What's the verdict?" Buller demanded.

"So damn much I can't really tell," Danny said, looking up mystified and rubbing his gleaming bald head. "All I know is we jest made a fortune stayin' to home an' gittin' drunk—an' mind, gittin' bloody well paid fer it." He pointed at the opposite wall. "Buller, quick, fetch a quart of Chicago hooch hid in one of Timmy's hip boots hangin' there. Timmy, here's a brand-new fly pole fer you— I'm stickin' with my ol' curtain rod. Swan, Taconite, do *somethin'*, goddamit. We gotta celebrate. My Gawd, we's jest made a fortune. We're rich, boys, *we're really rich!*"

9 *Kiss-and-Tell Fishermen*

Most fishermen swiftly learn that it's a pretty good rule never to show a favorite spot to any fisherman you wouldn't trust with your wife—a rule that possesses the further utility of narrowing the field fast. Show your secret Shangri-La to the wrong fisherman (mercifully, or at least so I've found it, they are still comparatively few) and the next time you visit the place you are more than apt to find *him* there ahead of you, quite often leading a guided tour.

Worse yet, if the place is really good and the character knows how to spell, chances are you'll soon be reading all about *his* intrepid new fishing discovery (meaning, of course, the fabled place *you* so foolishly showed him) in your favorite newspaper or outdoor magazine. For these are the compulsive squealers on good fishing waters who keep writing those glowing confessional articles one keeps reading, typically called "The Ten Best Trout Spots in Michigan" or "Monster Browns at Your Back Door"— usually accompanied by photos and detailed maps. And I'm not now

95

talking about those ill-disguised and often gaudily misin-
formed local-booster pitches, the main aim of which is to
fill local coffers rather than visiting creels, but rather of
hard, reliable dope about really hot fishing spots. These
latter are the charming kiss-and-tell fishermen to whom
I now give the back of my hand.

What it is that compels these strange characters to keep
snitching on good fishing spots, especially in writing and
to perfect strangers, has long baffled me. Fortunately for
the preservation of my own few remaining favorite spots,
I've never gotten to know one of these characters inti-
mately. Accordingly, I can only speculate that their odd
obsession must somehow accompany a particularly lardy
ego, one so driven by a primitive desire to show off and
be top rod at any price that its possessor is willing at one
swoop to kill both his reputation for piscatorial discre-
tion and the doomed spot he's just squealed on.

These kiss-and-tell fishermen must lead damn lonely
lives, one would guess, or else have to keep moving
around one hell of a lot in order to find a new batch of
sucker fishermen they can con into showing them still
newer spots to tell on. This is so because the normal
ordinary close-mouthed fisherman need only get
burned once in order to clam up and spread the alarm.

"Don't trust that squealing slob," runs some of his
milder idiom. "Last summer I foolishly showed him that
lovely pool below the third falls on the Middle Branch
and today it's nothin' but a goddam tourist mecca. Be-
ware of that flannel-mouthed mother-beatin' bastard an'
don't show him or tell him *nothin'*!"

The nicest thing I can offhand find to say about these
chronic kiss-and-tellers is that paradoxically they proba-

bly help save more good fishing spots than they ever ruin — though quite unintentionally, I hasten to add. This they do because their presence among us eventually makes the rest of us fishermen even more wary and suspicious and close-mouthed than nature has already so richly endowed us. This often means we grow slow to show our pet spots even to our tried and trusted fishing pals which naturally sharply reduces the fishing pressure on those remaining spots that have so far escaped the broadcasting flannel mouths.

Another thing the kiss-and-tellers unwittingly do is to make many of us fishermen far more likely to show our pet spots to visiting fishermen from far away than to some local worthies living on the same home grounds. One big reason is that it is far easier to hoodwink and figuratively blindfold a visiting stranger to where you are taking him than to fool a savvy local fisherman. That way, too, if the visiting stranger should turn out to be a flannel mouth, it needn't be quite so fatal as if he were a vocal local yokel, because he is far less apt to be able ever again to find the place, much less intelligently describe or identify it for others. Finally, should he nevertheless be able to find the spot again he simply won't be living so physically close to it and thus won't be around so often to help with its exposure and ultimate deflowering.

Consequently, one of the nicest compliments one local fisherman can pay another these days is to break down and actually show him a favorite spot. But even this generous gesture carries its hidden barb and it does so because if the shower fisherman can in fact trust the showee this means that henceforth the latter may never again honorably fish the place without the original shower tagging along as chaperone; either that or first giving his approval of a one-trip one-man sashay without him. Whereas if the showee *hadn't* been shown the lovely place, he just might — since both presumably haunt the same general fishing area — have stumbled across it on his own and thereafter been forever free as a bird to fish it whenever and with whomever he bloody well pleased. If this sounds a little tangled and complicated it's because it is; explaining the prevailing protocol at the Court of St. James's must be child's play compared with unraveling all the prickly nuances of the unwritten code of us crazy fishermen.

Possibly good old Hal had something like this in mind on that hot August afternoon a number of years ago when we were futilely fishing the lovely beaver dams on Anthony's Creek. As I kept vainly flailing away I became aware that Hal had stopped fishing and seemed to be watching me. At first I found his attention flattering, coming from such a savvy old master craftsman of angling, but as the surveillance continued I soon began miscasting in my nervous, glancing efforts to watch him watching me.

"What's up, Hal?" I finally said, giving up and reeling in. "You've been studying me as though you were Mr. Brinks weighing my application to drive one of your armored money vans. Did I make the grade?"

"In a way I was casing you, pal," Hal said, releasing his bomb. "How'd you like me to show you the hottest brook trout spot I know in Michigan?"

"Hal," I simpered, still in a state of shock, "that's like asking a soak if he'd mind inheriting a Kentucky distillery. When can we make the trip?"

98

"Right now, this very afternoon."

"You mean it's *that* close to here?"

"Follow me," Hal said, shaking his head. "And don't ask so damn many questions or I'll change my mind."

"Yessir," I said meekly, following Hal out to his four-wheel-drive fish car where we silently crawled out of our felt-soled diapers and took off, I feeling somewhat like a sheltered bride embarking on her first honeymoon: I suspected *something* real nice was going to happen to me real soon but precisely what it was I knew not.

Less than ten miles from the water we'd left, mostly over graveled country side roads, Hal stopped his bush car abruptly on a wooden bridge spanning a modest-sized stream. Several other fishy-looking cars were parked nearby, one of them bearing an out-of-state license. "Recognize the place?" he said.

"I think so, Hal," I said, quelling a low impulse to pretend I didn't. "Looks to me like the lingering remains of Strand Creek."

"Right," Hal said. "Fished it lately?"

"Not in years — ever since the tourists moved in," I said. "But I must confess I'm negotiating for the popcorn concession."

"Very funny. Where'd you used to fish it?"

"Downstream, Hal," I said, mystified over the prolonged cross-examination over a hatchery-planted stream I'd long ago abandoned to those wily angling detectives who prefer shadowing hatchery trucks. "Generally I'd shore-walk downstream and wade back fishing dry. Nice easy wading, but I finally got weary of catching hungry hatchery trout who'd rush up and fight over your fly."

99

"Hm . . . Ever try the water above?"

"Only once, Hal, and that was enough. Area gets real swampy and the stream narrows and dwindles fast. But the thing that really got me was crawling over and around and through all those slippery drowned cedars. That drove me up the wall — as well as fast back to my car."

"Plain chicken," Hal said, putting his car in gear. "That's the trouble with you lazy, unimaginative, rocking-chair fishermen. You just won't dream and explore anymore. Anyway, today you're again about to fish the Strand upstream."

"Yessir," I said, wincing over the prospect of once again tiptoeing terror stricken through the lovely downed cedars of Strand Creek. "Take me to your leader."

Less than a mile beyond the bridge Hal turned off on a bush-choked bumpy two-rut road, and thereafter creaked and bounced and wallowed along in four-wheel-drive until we ran out of road.

"Here we are," Hal announced, leaping out and grabbing at his fishing gear. "Let's get going."

"May I ask a question?" I timorously ventured.

"You just did," Hal said, "but live it up. Do ask another."

"Do we rig up here or pack in?"

"We pack in."

"Waders or hips?"

"Waders."

Once packed we took off, Hal in the lead, following no discernible trail but simply threading our way through dense stands of tamarack and spruce, which presently gave way to almost impenetrable cedar swamp broken by jungle clumps of tag alders. About the time I was ready to give the best trout spot in Michigan back to the Chippewa Indians we came into more open country dominated by poplars. Presently we were inching our way over and around the lush grassy tufts and mucky channels of once-flooded beaver meadows, a sure sign of the site of an ancient dam.

"Here we are," Hal said, pausing and pointing at an inky stretch of nondescript stream not more than two rod lengths wide from the surface of which protruded the bent trunks and rigid beseeching branches of a vast tangle of drowned cedars. Two blue herons suddenly rose from nowhere and undulantly flapped away in a sort of slow-motion oiled flight.

"Lovely place for an office picnic," I said. "Where do we launch the assault?"

"Right here," Hal said, plumping himself down on a fallen log. "As you can see, the place is fly-fishable only from this side. Moreover, the old stream channel's on the other side and 'way over your waders. Place is a real fooler."

"Sorta sweeps over me," I said, ruefully observing the tangle of grass and dangling bushes and overhanging brush that clotted the considerably higher limestone-layered opposite bank, the matted and tangled ruins of an inactive beaver dam some hundred feet below, and the more ominous fact that since we'd arrived there'd not been a single rise.

"What's that sound of running water I hear coming

from above?" I said, wrestling into my waders.

"Possibly the sound of running water," answered Hal, occasionally no mean slouch with the deflating riposte. "It's from a series of icy springs coming out of the limestone on the opposite bank. One reason the trout are here."

"*What* trout?" I wanted to ask but tactfully refrained, asking instead, "Where does one start fishing the hottest spot in Michigan?"

"Right in front of you, man," Hal said. "This is where the little darlings live."

"But how about you?" I said, noticing Hal still hadn't his waders on and was instead sitting back indolently smoking a cigar.

"I'll fish after you get bored and weary," Hal said airily. "Anyway, can't you see there's only room for one guy at a time? Get with it, dammit—we gotta get outa here before dark."

"Yessir," I said, snubbing up the knot on my little Adams and advancing a few steps to the water's edge and barely stepping in, catching my breath over the sudden shock of ice-cold water. From that point I fed out line and gracefully fouled my forward cast on some lurking brush and my fly slapped down upon the water with a thud scarcely a rod length above me. *Clap* went a savage flash of trout and I glanced back at Hal with the inimitable silly grin of a man who's just been cleaned out.

"See what you mean," I said, imaginatively tying on another Adams, which this time I promptly lost when an even larger trout immediately took it and made a quick power dive and broke me off on a submerged cedar.

"While they scarcely teach it in fly-casting classes," Hal

102

said, "you simply can't afford to posture and play around in these cedars with these muscular wild trout. You simply gotta skid 'em in fast as you can."

"Sweeps over me," I said, doggedly tying on another Adams.

I am not going to tell about all the gorgeous brook trout Hal and I caught and lost and broke off on that memorable evening, one reason being because we rapidly lost count. Virtually every cast with any kind of a fly ended in a savage strike, and we neither took nor saw any juniors though we did catch and return many close to and possibly over two pounds.

"Time's up," Hal announced after about a dizzy hour or so of the best trout fishing *I'd* ever seen in Michigan, at least since I was a kid. "Gotta quit now or we'll get caught in the dark. We'll return another day."

"Sorry," I said, reeling in. "I really can't make it till Tuesday."

On the slow trek out Hal told me how he'd first found the place. He'd done it the hard way, simply by slugging his way up from the bridge through all the down cedars until he'd come upon it. "Figured there just had to be some hot spots upstream with all that cold water and natural cover and, yes, protection from rival fishermen."

"Imagination pays," I said, "especially when it's accompanied by the stamina of a water buffalo and a suicidal disdain of all slippery cedars."

"Fact is, the first time I hit the place it looked so crummy and riseless I almost detoured around it," Hal ran on. "Fact is, some of the troutiest spots I've ever known looked the crummiest."

"Shows our illiterate native trout don't read the pretty

104

outdoor magazines," I said. "Good Lord, is it a mirage or a modern miracle and do I actually see your fish car?"

" 'Tis an authentic miracle and there's still another," Hal said. "How'd you like a slug of bourbon along with a dram of water out of an old tin cup?"

"To the best trout spot in Michigan and long may it reign," I said as we solemnly clinked cups. "And many thanks, pal, not only for showing me this gorgeous place but for your tacit if misguided testimonial to my character."

"I'll chance that, chum," Hal said.

Hal and I fished the best place in Michigan together on an average of about once a season after that, generally in the dog days of August. One reason we didn't fish it more often, perversely enough, was that the place was too damn easy, destroying the fisherman's ego-massaging illusion that his own guile and craft might sometimes affect the results. These trout would probably have as avidly hit a shoehorn.

But the biggest reason we didn't fish it oftener was our guilty if unspoken knowledge that in a sense these trout were trapped, driven and congregated there during hot weather and low water in their endless quest for food, cold aerated water, and some measure of security, just as I further suspect we managed to fish it at all because in our secret hearts we also knew that on this crowded planet fishermen and fish were both pretty much in the same boat.

The reign of the best place to fish in Michigan abruptly ended amidst the screaming whine and whimper of loggers' chain saws, we sorrowfully learned last August. While I was out of town Hal had hiked in there alone to

105

case the place for our annual trip and I got the bad news upon my return.

"I heard the wailing saws even from where we park the car," Hal explained in his bleak obituary report. "Most of the cedar is already gone and they're closing in on the spruce and tamarack, evidently sawing their way straight for Lake Superior."

"Did you try fishing the creek?" I managed to say.

"Lacked the heart," Hal said, sadly wagging his head. "When I got there and saw the old beaver dam full of trailer-camp suds and beer cans and floating garbage I almost knelt and wept. The loggers came in from the other side and have unerringly built a hauling bridge right over the hottest spot. From this bridge I beheld two immaculate characters spin casting and monotonously hauling in chubs. I didn't even rig up."

One final note: I want to take back my earlier innuendo that maybe Hal showed me this once-pristine place lest I'd find it first by myself. The truth is that *both* of us knew all along that never in this incarnation would I have ever slugged my way up through all those greasy down cedars and found it on my own. Instead I give thanks to Hal for giving me a fleeting glimpse of what the fishing still might be everywhere if it weren't for our helpless lust for "progress." Sometimes in the small hours of the night I think I even prefer kiss-and-tell fishermen. For the time at least we seem to have *them* outnumbered.

10 *Hoarding the Cast*

Fly-fishing for wild trout on quiet waters must be one of the toughest and craziest ways to catch fish ever invented by man, as well as among the most frustrating and humiliating. Yet, when the omens are right, it can also be the most exciting and rewarding. I know; I've got a bad case of it.

I've been haunting quiet waters, now that I look back on it, ever since my boyhood bait-plunking days—which means a powerful lot of quiet water over the dam. But only in recent years has it swept over me that what I long regarded as a harmless predilection is really a hopeless progressive disease and that I am deeply mired in its terminal stages.

My daily fishing notes tell the whole sad story, revealing that during the last two summers I have neither fished for nor caught anything but wild native brook trout—virtually none over twelve inches long and all taken on quiet waters while using scandalously long dreamy leaders with wee flies to match. My plight becomes all the more pitiable as I

contemplate all the pictures appearing lately in the local papers showing smirking piscatorial heroes all around me holding aloft almost equally burly rainbows or browns they have just derricked up or, when a block and tackle was handy, even vaster specimens of inert chinook or coho salmon—all of which I scorn.

In fact, so far sunk in sin am I that when people ask what I think of all the wondrous new fish that have invaded our waters, I am, if in a sufficiently liverish mood, apt to reply: "Simply dandy, buster. Just think of all the throngs of bait, hardware, and assorted meat fishermen these slobby new monsters are luring away from molesting my own precious troutlings."

During my long romance with quiet waters, mostly on small lakes and ponds and especially on virtually current-less beaver backwaters with which my Lake Superior country abounds, I naturally learned something about the hoarded cast. It was either that or no action, and action, I also gleaned along the way, is what this whole fly-fishing business is about. In addition I picked up some eloquent arguments to rebut the lying mythmaker who first started the rumor that our brookies are doomed because they are so easy to catch. Not while fly-fishing on quiet waters they ain't, mister, as this typical entry from my fishing notes shows: "Sunned out today. Fair rise but couldn't solve. Caught none and rose none." But before dilating further on the hoarded cast I must pause and pay my respects to the loyal order of flailers.

Flailers among fly-fishermen are so prolific that they defy accurate census, but one guesses they must be as plentiful as blackflies in August. A flailer, in case you never encountered one (or, worse yet, failed to recognize because you are one), is a fly-fisherman who casts too damn often and then compounds the felony by failing properly to fish out and retrieve the casts he makes. There are whole waterlogged regiments of them.

Speculating over what makes a flailer flail is as absorbing and, one suspects, ultimately as futile as trying to guess, say, why those queer quiet-water haunters got *their* way. Freud might have come up with some theories to make both types blush, but since he is unavailable for collaboration I must go it alone.

I have several pet theories, but my prize one is that since, under our droll economic system, the incipient flailer must, like most fishermen, work upwards of fifty weeks out of the year, once the poor pent devil finds himself actually unleashed on trout water he sort of cracks up or, to put it in more resonant five-dollar phrases, compulsively succumbs to an irresistible impulse to flail away. I call it my therapy theory of flailing.

At the risk of getting in over my intellectual waders I must unveil still another theory in which something more than simple stack-blowing therapy seems involved. It is this: Some flailers flail away so furiously that one suspects they must imagine they are beating up on someone, like maybe the boss. And I once beheld an oblivious flailer who flailed with such ecstatic abandon that I could have sworn he spied a seductive siren out there called Sade—wups, I mean Sadie—wearing only a Freudian slip.

Yet, however diversified their drives, flailers seem to share one thing in common: They all have a ball doing their thing; to a man they get a tremendous bang out of

109

the sheer manual act of casting. Along the way they also often acquire the physiques of weight lifters, which I suppose they must in order to keep up that old heave-ho all the livelong day. Actually, they are a remarkable race of fishermen and whenever I feel a little impatient with them I recall that I too love the physical act of fly-casting, and in fact once even wrote a piece celebrating its delights that opened thus: "Fly-fishing is such great fun, I have often felt, that it really ought to be done in bed."

Flailers share one other thing in common: They rarely raise, much less ever catch, a trout. Watching one at his devotionals swiftly reveals why. After resolutely stomping up to the water he will so shortly rid of all trout, your typical flailer strips out line like an overworked barber whipping up a cold lather. Then suddenly he braces himself and lifts the accumulated mass and blindly flings it out yonder as far as he can. Then, before his fly has fairly landed, he retrieves the whole whirling mess and whales her out again. This goes on all day.

After a spell of watching such an awesome performance —*whish, plop, wheek*— one wonders if the flailer could possibly rid the area of trout any faster if he whipped out a pistol and fired into the water. It could make an exciting race. Carrying on this way it is little wonder that so few trout ever disturb a flailer's reveries. The main reason they don't, of course, is that they are no longer there, my latest research disclosing that a really distinguished flailer can chase every decent trout into the next township by, at most, his third cast.

If I seem to be trying to reform our grand army of flailers, I really don't mean to; first, because I doubt they can or want to be reformed, and second, because I regard them as among our most ardent trout conservationists and wouldn't change them for the world. Nor am I poking fun at them, either, for in solemn truth they should be toasted rather than roasted. So let's lift a glass to our hardy flailers, a noble breed of abstentious souls who so rarely ever raise a trout, let alone take one home. After all, think of all the trout they save!

If the very fishermen who stand most in the need of the hoarded cast are beyond redemption, then, as I've just implied, to whom *does* it apply? Could it possibly apply, say, to such suave and crafty old fly-fishing hands as you and I, who cast with such consummate grace and precision, and who invariably work our fly out of the magic hot spot before going into our lift retrieve?

The answer, alas, is yes; the hoarded cast applies to you and me and to all other wistful souls who fish the fly. In fact I sometimes suspect that a failure to use the strategy of the hoarded cast may be the biggest single lack in the arsenal of most otherwise competent fly casters. The merest glance at some of the unique problems facing the fly-fisher should show what I'm driving at.

Fly-fishing is first of all a combined act of high deceit and low fakery aimed at creating the illusion that a bent pin adorned with assorted fluff is something good to eat. Next, nothing good to eat in a trout's natural habitat comes equipped with a strange light-refracting gut or synthetic tail at least seven feet long. If I've made sense so far than it follows as the night the day that a fly-fisherman should do only those things that heighten his illusion and disguise his fakery, which, in turn, put

111

another way, revolves around his eternal battle with light.

Though there are few rules in fishing that nose-thumbing trout haven't riddled with exceptions at one time or another, if any ironclad rules do exist my guess is that high on the list is one running something like this: Light is the most constant problem facing the fly-fisherman and glaring sunlight is the worst possible light he has to face. The reason, of course, is that the stronger the light the weaker the illusion, and by definition glaring sunlight is the glarin'est. Which is probably why virtually all fly-fishermen pray less for salvation than for solid overcast.

Why their prayers are so seldom answered is a question vexing experts, some claiming that God conducts an impartial head count and there are simply more tourists praying the other way. In any case, during the average trout season a fly-fisherman is lucky to draw one really overcast day out of ten. So unless he stays home and sulks the other nine or else takes up night fishing (which I happen personally to abhor), he must on most days bravely sally forth in the jolly sunshine prepared to battle his enemy Light.

But how does he fight light? one may ask. The answer is by waiting. Waiting for what? Waiting for any number of things. Like what? Well, waiting for a passing cloud bank to come obscure the sun; waiting for a breeze to spring up and create a protective ripple; waiting for a bank of fog or mist or even smog; waiting for a gentle shower; in short, waiting for anything that will help heighten his illusion and hide his fakery. But what if nature fails to cooperate? Then he simply sighs and ties on a finer tippet and commands himself to wait longer between casts, always slowly retrieving the fly virtually to his feet before going into the pickup. He practices, in short, the discipline of the hoarded cast.

The hoarded cast, then, is not a method of casting but a method of not casting; not something the fisherman should do but something he shouldn't do. Its whole rationale is bottomed upon trying to circumvent or mitigate the illusion-shattering hazard of light. It is a doctrine of restraint and self-discipline, of simple waiting and biding one's time. It is to take it slow and easy; that is, to use the hoarded cast. One of these fine sunny days I think I'll even try it.

11 *The Ways of Fishermen*

The longer I fish the stronger I feel that one way to get the dope on a man fast is to watch him fish; it swiftly separates the men from the boys. I mean not only watching his technique or lack of it and actual manner of casting and the like, but looking for less obvious but possibly more subtle clues to the inner man, such as how he handles a fish, once caught, including how he removes and returns it (*if* he returns it) as well as observing such loftier portents as his approach and general attitude toward his fishing and indeed toward the whole outdoors.

I should warn that you may not find too many fish on your line watching other men trying to get fish on theirs, but you will, if you can interpret what you see (next season I'll explain all about *that*, advance orders now being taken at your favorite laundromat), get a pretty good line on the character you bother to watch.

And since I like also to bandy with the idea that there must be almost as many kinds of fishermen abroad in the land as there are fishermen (something like fingerprints), I guess what I'm really saying is that fishermen are just about as mixed a breed of cats as the rest of mankind. One need only look to find all kinds and types, ranging from spiritual descendants of Henry Thoreau on down to the most hopeless fishing hogs.

This latter-day view of mine clashes sharply with a dream I once cherished that there just *had* to be a little good in every fisherman. This boyish pipedream vanished in a cloud of profanity and disillusion about the time I first had to forsake my own fishing to remove from crystal trout waters I intended to fish the appalling avalanche of cans and bottles and assorted offal flung there by a descending horde of barbarians who called themselves fishermen . . .

For in the realm of fishing, as elsewhere, one can't have it both ways; if it's really true that fishermen vary like other men, which I now firmly believe, then it follows as the day the night that while some fishermen may indeed occasionally dally with the angels, just as surely others will turn out to be certified slobs and authentic sonsabitches. Thus, merely describing a person as a fisherman reveals no more about him than does the color of his eyes. If you really want to know what makes the bastard tick you must watch him fish, an experience as revealing as the ultimate verdict is often hard to put in words.

This sudden rash of metaphysical speculation, piscatorial division, is prompted by nothing more profound than a desire to say a few words about an interesting man I periodically fish with. I bring him up because our fishing together may prove, if indeed it proves anything, that kindred fishermen quickly recognize each other and

115

that this recognition forms a bond of toleration for their differences perhaps rarely found, much less ever equaled, in other pastimes or walks of life.

The man's name is Ed Lotspeich and he lives in a distant southern Ohio town where he works for a large soap company, and in fact is a wheel in the outfit. Ed and I met a dozen-odd years ago under circumstances that slip my mind, and ever since then we fish up here together every summer, rarely for more than a couple of days, following which a presumably fortified and renewed Ed returns to his chores until another year.

The point of my even mentioning this rather casual fishing relationship is that I can offhand think of few of my fishing pals more unlike each other in so many non-fishing ways as Ed and I are—and yet we hit it off. Whether the subject be political, economic, military, industrial, or whatever, we seem to be whole light-years apart. In fact we fail to see eye to eye on virtually everything men can find to talk about, not involving fishing, including those two vast wastelands in which Ed's work keeps him up to his ears, television and advertising (win a new washer by guessing my size!), and mighty are our arguments as we drive across the countryside declaiming on the modern drift of that ancient dream called democracy. Yet once we start fishing, our clashing swords turn magically into fairy bamboo wands as we wordlessly fish hour after blissful hour . . .

For, as you've already guessed, the one big thing on which Ed and I *do* agree is our fishing. In fact after much profound pondering I can't think of another fisherman among all those I've ever known—and that's been an awesome crew—who fishes more my way and I his than

117

Edgar H. Lotspeich and yours truly. And should you think I've simply cowed the man into submission then you don't know brother Ed or haven't seen or heard us in action when we don't agree. For the simple truth is that Ed and I, for all our differences, love to fish the same places in the same way at the same pace—a rare phenomenon among anglers, as any crusty old fisherman will quickly tell you.

In saying this I don't mean to imply that our way is the only way, or the better way, or the more virtuous way, or the flower-strewn way to catching more fish or having more fun. Not even faintly. All I am trying to say is that we curious fisherfolk fish for many things in many ways; that we quickly spot any kindred souls, and that this mutual shock of recognition forms a powerful, forgiving bond even if in other areas we may be poles apart. (No pun intended, this I swear, since any self-respecting fly-fisherman would sooner be caught dead than ever call his rod a pole.) Nor do I imply that men must fish alike in order to hit it off, because I know dozens of misguided souls I have a ball fishing with who wouldn't fish my way for all the oil in Araby, or I theirs.

Just what Ed's and my way of fishing is I'd better not try to capture in a closing paragraph, especially after writing three books trying to explain the mystery to myself. But whatever that way is, Ed and I happily share it; it is the one big unspoken thing that seems to dissolve our differences and make them seem trivial; for it is, I suspect, the elusive something that keeps me looking forward to Ed's annual visits and, I choose to think, keeps good old Ed coming back.

12 *Trout Magic*

Fate, aided by the successful conclusion of my brewer-grandfather's long search for a community simply crawling with permanently parched beer guzzlers, planted me in a glaciated northern Michigan iron-mining town not far from Lake Superior. To call our Upper Peninsula weather variable is an act of charity; one comes closer by misquoting what Mark Twain once said about his native Hannibal, "If you don't like the weather around here, buster, just wait five minutes."

One of the few predictable things about our U.P. weather, in fact, is that in winter a person is lucky even to glimpse the sun once in ten days, while in summer it's just the other way around. Then the sun seems permanently glued to a cloudless sky. All this is fine for tourists seeking cheek of tan, no doubt, but rough on us native fishermen, especially on those oddballs among us who prefer to stalk our trout on quiet waters. There, to put it mildly, a burning sun is one of the most dependable omens of piscatorial disaster.

Although I long ago learned my

glare-sun lesson I nevertheless continued to fight it, stubbornly whipping my sun-drenched ponds into a yeasty froth rivaling that on grandpa's beer. From this I learned at least one memorable lesson: that neither stamina nor the number of casts a fisherman contrives to make have much to do with either the art or the material success of fly-casting.

I was long aware, of course, that I might greatly have eased my glare-sun problems by fishing only in the evenings, and "finally taking leave of the solitary angler at eventide" — as the man with the tremulous voice in the old movie travelogues might have put it — "fishing, ever casting into the fading afterglow." All this I knew. And I also knew that sundown is one of the most dreamily beautiful times of any northern summer day and that some of the most dramatic rises occur then.

Nevertheless I persisted in fishing during the daylight hours every chance I got until, in recent years, I have virtually given up all evening fishing. One reason is that I've fallen too much in love with fishing to wait around all day to go pay it court. Another, I guess, is that for too many years I simply had to do most of my fishing at night. Another is that by the end of a long day I'm usually too pooped to tackle it again. Another is that I've discovered the remarkable therapy lurking in a few late-afternoon belts of bourbon, following which I've grown afraid even to unjoint one of my precious fly rods, much less risk groping my way waterward euphorically brandishing it. Moreover, too much postbourbon exertion, I've found, gives me the hiccups—*wheek!*—which in turn throws off my timing. Try it sometime . . .

The irony, you see, was double. The more time I

120

found for fishing coincided with a growing passion for going at it the least favorable time of day; that is, during the peak hours of a high-riding glare sun. But there I was, stuck with it, and on many days I proudly counted not the trout I caught but the few tentative sashays I got at my fly. Sashays were awfully good, I soon discovered, rolled in cornmeal and fried in bacon grease. So with the advance in years, if not precisely in wisdom, I looked for other things to do to while away the more resolutely riseless hours and avoid the risk of ever becoming bored with my greatest outdoor love.

These antiboredom diversions were few at first but presently grew and grew. Chief among them was gathering wild berries and cherries as their seasons occurred, ranging from the delicious early highbush berries known locally as either sugarplums or Juneberries, a helpless passion for which I share with the bears, on to the late-autumn wild cranberries; gathering all manner of wild mushrooms ranging from the delicate spring morel to the indescribably delicious late-summer *Boletus edulis* (as well as gathering a small ambulant library to reduce the Russian roulette aspects of eating them); picking bouquets of wild flowers in an effort to placate a certain fisherman's wife; exploring for likely new spots to fish; sometimes just taking a Thoreauvian tramp in the woods.

Two summers ago, thanks to a gift from Charles Kuralt when he was up here adding this fisherman to his "On the Road" collection of mavericks and assorted oddballs, I added a new toy to my fishing diversions: a tape recorder for tracking down the myriad marvelous sounds one hears while out fishing—shrilling frogs,

121

droning insects, all manner of bird calls, the occasional far-off wail of a coyote.

My biggest prize so far is the plaintive call of a white-throated sparrow (the "lonely bird," I like to call it) mingling with that of a faraway train whistle, the haunting sound of which would chill the spine of a mummy. Then last summer I stumbled upon a fascinating new diversion, in turn inspired by what has long remained my strangest fishing trip, both of which I shall presently unveil. But first a word, as the TV peddlers say, on how a guy can possibly do all these other things and still occasionally cast a fly.

2

Just as I rarely fish all day anymore, even on the best days, so I rarely fail to fish at least several hours, even on the worst. And since I go out fishing virtually every day all day all summer long (after my morning session of cribbage, that is), this gives me plenty of time for all that and fishing too, as the saying goes. One fairly obvious reason for my tapering off on my fishing is that I tire easier, I suppose, but I prefer to think it's mostly because I'm no longer as mad at the trout as I used to be. In fact I'm not mad at them at all anymore, and could, if pressed, think of quite a few fishermen I'd rather see removed from our streams, especially those engaging types who regard any daily creel limit as a minimum goal the achievement of which is a continuing challenge to their manhood rather than a warning to stop their swinery.

This does not mean I've gone soft on fishing, heaven

forbid, and now prefer prowling the woods weaving garlands of ground pine to adorn my graying locks. Perish the thought, Piscator (if you're listening), because I've remained faithful to thee in my fashion, I swear, and am in fact steadily getting worse. Far from forsaking fishing, then, I prefer to think I've fallen so madly in love with it that I'm like the devoted loverboy who so adores his lady he simply can't bring himself to keep pestering and pawing away at her when he knows she's not in the mood.

This change of heart toward my fishing has brought other changes, and at the risk of getting shot by certain local chambers of commerce I must also reveal that I no longer make my ritual annual fishing treks to far places, places like Canada and the Far West. It must be twenty years now since my last safari to that magical old logging dam off the Algoma Central Railroad in Ontario where, on the first cast I ever made there, an erupting cone of glorious trout came rushing up fighting for my fly. What finally cast a chill over our romance was the horrendous time when, at the very same spot, three of us failed to raise a legal trout in as many days.

It wasn't so much the humiliation that bugged me and opened my eyes to the delights of staying home but the dramatic proof that there are times on even the most fabled fishing waters when all hell and Izaak Walton can't raise a decent trout. About the same time it swept over me that when the fishing is good at these remote spots it's apt to become a bloody bore and that when it's bad it's too damned far to go to get skunked. One can do *that* quite nicely at home, thank you, not to mention all the money one can save to squander on new gear and old bourbon. From my Ontario trauma emerged

123

Traver's Law, which I generously pass along, lurching syntax and all: When the fishing's lousy travel ain't gonna help it and when it's good a guy don't need to. But I do miss the colorful old Algoma Central . . .

Despite all these diversions and withdrawal symptoms I still manage to fish every day, come hell or high sun. This I do not from any sense of duty or out of pained courtesy to a waning love. No. I still fish because I love to, because I love the very act of fly-casting, which seems to do for me what her daily pirouettes before her lonely mirror doubtless do for a retired ballerina. Moreover, fly-fishing seems to me to be the world's most painless way to get some exercise and, one might say, inadvertently keep in shape, perhaps a trifle less invigorating than those daily romps around the reservoir my jogging city brothers make, but possibly more fun.

But most of all I am endlessly fascinated by the lure of the unexpected and unknown, probably inherent in all forms of fishing, and in experimenting with offbeat flies and nymphs, mostly tiny. And constantly I pursue what is perhaps the fisherman's wildest dream, the perfect leader. Wild because the perfect leader, I suppose, would not only need to be perfectly invisible but strong enough to stand the strike of a decent trout. My continued pursuit of this elusive will-o'-the-wisp is not in order to catch more fish, I virtuously add, but in the wistful hope that once in a blue moon a mere mortal fisherman might fool the sun.

In recent years it has increasingly occurred to me, especially on my birthdays, that any advantages that lurk in growing old seem largely to have eluded me. Possibly one of them, however, is the leisure the phenomenon

124

gives an older fisherman to fish the way he wants and at his own pace. This not only adds surprisingly to the joy and fun of fishing but gives the fisherman a chance to look around. And the longer I fish the surer I am that one of the special fascinations of going fishing at all is the strange and wonderful sights a fisherman can see if only he'll look about him.

This repose to look around is not given to all fishermen, more's the pity, for under our droll economic system it seems most fishermen have to work. And this distracting circumstance in turn puts most fishermen under one of society's harshest pressures, the inexorable pressure of time. This tyranny takes many forms, of course: the pressure to squeeze the last drop out of an ebbing vacation or a fleeing weekend or the pressure of knowing he's running late for that date with a girl friend, or his boss, or a customer or client or hot prospect—the list is endless—or possibly even with his own wife.

All of us have encountered such poor, pressurized fishermen on the stream, each with his intent catatonic stare, a rod-waving automaton casting as if by metronome, so oblivious of all about him he doubtless wouldn't look away if a herd of water buffalo came charging out of the woods. These harried souls occasionally catch a fish, no doubt, but at the cost of missing so very much.

Most of the sights they miss usually involve some sort of wild flora or fauna, naturally, and my daily fishing notes (which I've kept for nearly forty years) abound with scribbled records of the offbeat sights I've seen. For example, I've long ago lost count of all the bears I've run across—and occasionally almost into—many of these encounters seeming quite hilarious to look back on but none being the least bit funny, I swear, at the tense uncertain moment they occurred.

I could also run on for hours about the birds and bees and other flying things I've caught while casting, mostly back when I fished at night, including one mammal, of all things. Before I'm called a liar I should explain that my mammal was only one mighty scared bat, almost as scared as I was in releasing him—*snip*—along with a favorite fly.

Most fishermen, being human, naturally prefer re-counting their little triumphs rather than their many failures—as our outdoor magazines so regularly and richly prove. All of which suggests one further small advantage in growing old, for by then a fisherman will likely have been overtaken by a measure of candor, and moreover have caught so many trout his surfeited ego will at last let him occasionally reveal some of the times he fell on his ass. What follows, then, is an account of one of my more epic piscatorial pratfalls. Part of its charm lies in the fact that if the fishing *had* been good that day, al-most certainly I would have missed my strangest fishing experience. For both happened on the same trip, one right after the other. It was a busy day.

3

It was a warm bright day in late August as I floated downriver in my little cedar boat, occasionally dipping my paddle to avoid a rock or deadhead or, when the spirit moved, making a languid cast or two at a likely looking spot. But mostly I floated lazily along, drinking in the unfolding sights, enjoying the drowsy illusion that the boat itself was tethered while the landscape glided by, reveling in the trancelike float down this lovely new river —new to me, that is. Some of the leaves were already turning color, flashing and rustling in the breeze like tiny tambourines, the caressing breeze itself feeling soft as the down under a starling's wing.

Only one small canker marred the enchantment of my float: I'd been at it for several hours and had yet to see a rising trout. Now scenic floats were doubtless fine for poets with notebooks, I told myself; prosaic fishermen crave occasionally to see a fish . . . As I rounded another slow bend I surprised a drinking doe with two spunky fawns, and I longed for my Brownie as I watched them prance across the river in a watery halo and off and away into the woods. That made at least a dozen deer I'd already seen, I figured, besides the flash of a red fox as well as scores of scolding local ducks resenting my intrusion. But *I'd* come here to fish, not to hunt or conduct a game census, so before I reached the next bend I resolved that if there wasn't some action before the next succeeding bend I'd turn myself around and hook up the putt-putt and, my supply of shear pins willing, get the hell out of there.

"One more bend," I promised myself, at the same time vowing never again to listen to any hot tips from the lips of bragging fellow anglers. "Nevermore," I ran on, snitching a favorite word from Poe, "nevermore in this incarnation will this fisherman ever bounce his way through umpteen malarial bogs on the mere tavern-inspired word of some mouthy fellow angler. *Nosiree!*"

By the time I'd completed my vows of abstinence

127

(which I've repeated so often before and since), I'd rounded the decisive bend and there, leaning far out across the broad river, I saw a giant old white pine clinging precariously to a steep flood-eroded bank. The sight prodded my memory and I grabbed for the hurried notes I'd made as my tipster had spun his trouty fantasies. "When you reach the big leaning pine," they read, "quick drop anchor—the hot spot's just below that at the mouth of a nameless feeder creek." So I quick dropped anchor and again squinted at my notes. "Don't float near the feeder creek," they ran on, "because that's the hottest spot where the trout are specially big and wild and spooky. Instead, beach your boat and wade into range. Easy does it."

Trembling with a sudden attack of that fisherman's incurable virus, eternal optimism, I stashed my notes and grabbed my paddle to push ashore. Then, for the first time, I saw I'd floated dangerously close to the hottest hot spot. I wheeled around and was charmed to spy my anchor rope floating gaily far upriver and quickly confirmed that one of my favorite knots had come unraveled for perhaps the first time since Scouting days. Facing front again I saw to my horror that meanwhile I'd floated squarely into the very mouth of the feeder creek. I leaned and peered overboard, whereupon all hell broke loose.

For a frozen instant it seemed the shallow creek bottom was paved with quiescent trout; then, presto, the pavement broke up and came alive and the place was suddenly aswarm with dozens and scores of gorgeous speckled trout crazily darting and dashing every which way, reminiscent of those wild cops-and-robbers chases in the early movies or, to be a bit more moderne, like some surrealist scene in the addled dreams of one thoroughly stoned fisherman. As I stared and stared I felt my boat grate gently ashore and when next I looked all the trout had vanished.

If, as I suspect, there are few goofs a fisherman forgives more readily than his own, then I rose bravely to the occasion. "Probably couldn'ta caught 'em anyway," I consoled myself. "Some days a guy can't ketch 'em in a hatchery." My wounded pride thus appeased I mentally shrugged and lit an Italian cigar and sat there meditatively puffing away. As the clouds of smoke billowed forth and the mosquitoes sensibly fled I recalled it was my old fishing pal Luigi who'd taught me that *these* made the very best fly dope around. I also recalled that only my own persistence further taught me that all that keeps Italian cigars from becoming the universal fly dope is not any question whether the flies can't stand them but whether the fisherman can . . .

In my mood of self-forgiveness I even forgave my tipster for sending me on this wild goose chase. "After all, the trout *were* here," I indulgently conceded, "just like the man said. After all, I can't blame *him* for a little accident with a lousy anchor rope. Could happen to anybody."

I dipped my fingers idly in the feeder creek and quickly withdrew them, the water was so unbelievably cold. I looked at my watch and then up at the cloudless noontide sky. What to do, what to do? Far too early to quit fishing and far too late to go elsewhere. Hm . . . About then it occurred to me that all these trout couldn't possibly have been ganged up here simply for the food.

129

Surely part of the lure must have been the concentration of cold aerated water after a long hot summer. Hm . . . If so, why couldn't there be more speckled lovelies farther up this unknown stream? True, it was a little narrow and brushy down here but, who knew, maybe there were open meadows and even working beaver dams farther on up. Why not bestir yourself, master knot tyer, and go take a look?

The going was slow at first because of the tangle of tag alders, which soon got so bad—and I so hot and winded —that I took down my rod and waded the gravelly creek itself, grateful for the sudden clutch of cold water around my steaming hip boots. I made better time after that and presently the alders thinned enough so I could make out a low, sparsely wooded ridge looming on my right which I headed for, guessing the creek and ridge might follow each other and the latter prove easier going.

At least it was cooler up on the ridge and for the first time I saw that its topmost crest was composed of a drab darkish-looking rock ledge—some sort of coarse-grained schist, I guessed—in turn virtually covered by a minute lichen which made the ledge seem mysteriously to merge with the tangle of growth below. Farther down the ridge I could also see countless rock fragments scattered helter-skelter almost down to the creek, rocks sheared from the mother ledge over the course of many years, I guessed. Despite the maze of fallen rocks, I found the going was better than fighting tag alders, so I stayed up on the ridge, rarely losing sight of the brushy creek. Presently the ledge and the creek grew closer together and I stopped short and stared, for there below me lay a vast ancient beaver meadow.

Several things testified to its antiquity: mature trees growing among the hummocky tufts of sun-bleached grass outlining the old backwater; the rarely discernible old dam itself, now little more than a long-overgrown serpentine mound like the burial ground of a prehistoric monster; the lack of any vestige of backwater, the narrow creek dancing along down to the river much as it must have ever since the last glacier.

For a long time I stood marveling over what a magnificent dam and pond this must once have been, not to mention glorious fishing. But there was exploring to do so I pushed on up the ridge, still looking, and abruptly tripped and fell on my face. "At least I spared the rod *and* the fisherman," I thought after I'd scrambled up and run out of profanity and stood glaring down at the cause of my fall—a curiously concentrated pile of rocks. "Funny thing," I thought, staring accusingly at it, "if I weren't so far out in the brambles I'd swear somebody piled these damn rocks here on purpose." For indeed it seemed that, however crudely, someone had once deliberately fashioned a low wall of rock between the mother ledge and the creek bottom.

I shrugged and slowly pushed on, wary of hidden rock traps, and in less than a dozen paces abruptly came upon still another half-hidden and even larger pile of lichen-covered rocks. This time there was no mistake: *Men* had piled these rocks here, carefully, deliberately, one upon another, so that they formed a kind of low rocky fortress facing the creek. I also noted that the

131

downstream end lay open, possibly for quick exodus, while the upstream end curved around either to afford protection from or to block the view of anyone coming downstream.

A large fallen tree, so rotted I couldn't tell what kind it was, lay across this fort, and generations of pine needles and fallen leaves and other natural detritus nearly filled the crude structure. Without considerable digging there was no way of telling how high and deep it must once have been, but I offhand guessed it could have accommodated at least a score of men. "Crouching, armed men," I concluded after further staring, suddenly discovering I was shivering.

I looked at my watch and saw the afternoon was slipping away so I resolved to abandon all thoughts of fishing or exploring above and shed my gear and confine my looking to this curious area. That way, too, I'd be surer of getting out of the spooky place before dark. Once again I found myself shivering so I quickly pushed on, reflecting how rapidly our northern autumn days were apt to cool.

Within the next fifty yards I came upon three more forts, all similarly fashioned and each facing the old beaver meadow as well as being protectively curved at the upstream end, the last fort overlooking the top margin of the old beaver meadow. Still I pushed on for maybe another quarter mile, gripped by a chilled fascination over what I was finding. Though the low rocky ledge and fallen rocks still persisted I found no more forts. Several things now seemed to be emerging: These forts rather clearly had been built when the big beaver pond was still there and, whatever their significance, the destinies of the two seemed fatefully interlocked.

Retracing my steps I quickly gathered up my gear and hurried down to the creek. There I turned for a farewell look at the forts and made a further startling discovery: none of the five rocky forts I had so recently all but stumbled over could now be seen, not the faintest trace. Not only had they been built by men, I saw in a flash, but diabolically fashioned to merge with the rock ledge behind them when viewed from below.

Shivering, I turned and all but fled the place, my mind so churning with morbid speculations that when I reached the big river I forgot to fish. Instead I hastily clapped on my motor and raced upriver, scattering ducks and deer, miraculously shearing only three propeller pins before I reached my bush car and the solace of a couple of shots of bourbon.

I have now told about my strangest fishing trip, one that has haunted me for years—nearly thirty, I'd guess—during which many are the theories I've spun and brooded to explain why those forts were ever there and what might have happened. Gradually, one theory has emerged, and as soon as I clap on my archeologist wig I'll reveal it. Meanwhile skeptics will please form a line on the left.

4

Perhaps the quickest way to launch my main theory is to state at the outset that I no longer regard these crude rock structures as forts at all in any defensive sense; rather I see them as cleverly placed and craftily camouflaged temporary hiding places from which to launch a sudden surprise attack.

Attack upon whom?

Unsuspecting people coming downstream from above, probably in canoes.

How can you tell?

Because each "fort" was so carefully curved at the upstream end, remember, not so much for defense, in my view, but to avoid alerting the intended victims by possible discovery of the hidden attacking forces.

Seems these "temporary" structures lasted pretty long. How come?

I call them temporary because obviously they were so crudely and hurriedly put together, possibly under cover of darkness,. and would today doubtless be the despair of any self-respecting stonemason. A companion theory I bandy with, though, is that the crudeness may have been deliberate because if they had been more formally and carefully built they might thereby have lost their camouflage and thus the important element of surprise. In any case, the fact that they still stand is to my mind mute proof that the attack richly succeeded.

What do you mean?

Look, if many or even any of the victims of this attack survived this epic massacre, which must have become legendary, they or their descendants almost certainly would have returned and destroyed these forts to prevent their ever again being used against them. In my view the few if any terrified survivors fled the dreaded area never to return. This view in turn is some negative evidence that the victims themselves might originally have been invaders, since people don't lightly forsake their native grounds.

134

But why build any forts at all? Why didn't the waiting

attackers simply lie up on the rocky bluff behind them and leisurely pick off their victims with rifles?

Because I more and more think these forts were built before firearms reached this area, possibly even back in pre-Columbian times—which after all is but the wink of an eye in the long history of man.

Then they'd have had to have been native American Indians, wouldn't they?

Who else? Leif Ericsson and his boys?

Don't be funny. All right, if they were Indians who were actually living there before the age of firearms, why didn't they use the trusty bow and arrow, which my dictionary tells me predates even Christopher?

Because some of the intended victims might thus have escaped. The more I ponder this whole puzzling thing the more I'm convinced that this was a cold, calculated savage man-to-man combat, with total obliteration as the only goal, fought at close quarters with primitive weapons: spears, tomahawks, stone hatchets and axes, possibly even with clubs.

But why so mad at their victims?

I've already touched on that, though I have several guesses. Chief among them are that the victims were really the invaders who had earlier taken over or dared trespass on coveted hunting or fishing or trapping grounds upstream, a theory I rather lean to. Another, less likely, one is that the attackers were the usurpers. Still another is that it was an intertribal struggle for power or, for the more romantically inclined, the favor of some dusky maiden.

All your various theories envisage a considerable party of descending canoeists. Wouldn't they also have been

135

armed and, if so, how come they were such sitting ducks?

That's the five-dollar question that most bothers me. One guess is that the attackers polished off each group of canoeists as it hit the beaver pond and then hid again and waited for another batch to come along. Another more likely guess is that it was the practice of groups of native canoeists to congregate in full force before making any downstream portage, especially in exposed areas, and that the waiting attackers knew this. In any case the victims, however heavily armed, had naturally to leave their canoes before making any portage over the dam. This was probably the moment of truth when the attackers struck.

But would such a large party of canoeists likely make a crowded portage all at once into one narrow stream below the big dam?

Scarcely, but my guess is that the lower forts struck as the first portages began, the upper ones closing in to cut off any attempted upstream retreat.

But couldn't these "forts" have merely been primitive hunting blinds?

Five large game blinds would not likely exist in such small compass and hold such an army of "hunters." Even our most imaginative U.P. chambers of commerce don't claim our hunting is *that* good. Nor would mere game blinds have likely been made of heavy rock.

But doesn't that fact alone blast your offensive theory?

Not at all. The forts simply had to be made of rock because the presence of any other kind of contrived structures, whether of grass or logs or freshly dug earth, would have instantly been obvious to the thus-alerted descending boatmen.

You're wearing me down, old fisherman. Have you ever been back?

Yes, last summer.

Forts still there?

Yes, but now even more overgrown and hard to find.

How about any fishing above?

Didn't find any, though I prowled for miles. Only a maze of alder-choked feeder creeks and vast, ruined beaver dams. Once must have been glorious, though. Mainly I went there to confirm or confound my latest guesses.

Which won?

Mostly they were confirmed.

Please enlighten the groping canaille.

Well, I scoured the whole area with my latest toy, a brand-new electronic metal detector, and found not a trace.

So what?

Seems pretty strong negative evidence that this massacre must have happened before the age of metal. Surely during such a bloody melee as I envisage somebody would have dropped a rifle or powder horn or at least a knife or hatchet. Yet I raised nary a whisper.

Maybe your detector was haywire.

Possibly, but it has worked like a charm before and ever since.

My, my. Ever find anything interesting?

All depends what you call interesting. No twenty-dollar gold pieces, if that's what you mean.

You name it, then.

Well, my own biggest find so far is the melancholy conviction that any future archeologists whose ancestors

137

miraculously survive our present age of slobbery will be forced to conclude that our civilization perished in a torrential hail of beer cans.

Anything else, you funny man?

Plenty, but right now, if you'll please kindly excuse me, I think I'll go fishing—I think I see a rise out yonder. Or maybe it's just another flying beer can. It's getting so an old fisherman can't always tell anymore. Sometimes, in fact, I wish I were born a hundred years B.B.C.

You mean before Christ or that English broadcasting outfit?

Neither, comrade—I mean back in the pastoral days *before beer cans.*

13 *Morris the Rodmaker*

Fly rods are like Cornish pasties—both are best made for love rather than for money. And where love is missing the cost of the rod is often irrelevant. I've owned several expensive "name" rods that turned out to be magnificent tent poles, and one of the loveliest rods I ever owned was a dreamy old prewar Granger that cost a mere twenty-five bucks. (It now stands retired in my den window cross-sworded with a gallant old Paul Young.) While most good fly rods are also expensive, alas, without care and love one can easily wind up flailing a mere ornate broomstick. All of which brings me to Morris the Rodmaker.

Morris Kushner and I first met when he stopped off one summer while driving to Montana on a fishing trip. He'd spent the night at our town's only hotel, having driven the day before from his suburban home near Detroit—almost as far from where I live, believe it or not, as I in turn live from Hudson's Bay.

So the next morning all Morris had to do to find me was to walk across the street to the Rainbow Bar, where I'd earlier written him he might find me if I wasn't home. I was absorbed playing cribbage when he walked in, but since we small-towners always case every stranger, when I glanced up at Morris I saw what I guessed was a retired bourbon-bibbing Irish railroad man: sturdy, ruddy, blue eyed, smiling, cigar smoking and radiating a kind of tolerant good will.

I can't recall whether I won or lost at cribbage that morning, though I must say, like most fishermen, I tend to forget my bad days. Anyway, when the game was over Morris came over and introduced himself (I never did ask him how he recognized me) and we had a draft beer and naturally I asked him if his travel plans allowed him a few hours off to join me in fishing. "Do they, Mr. Kushner?" I repeated.

"Of course," he said, removing his stogie with the loving reluctance of the inveterate cigar smoker. "And don't keep mistering me, old fisherman, 'cause we aren't all that far apart."

"Righto, Morris," I said. "Let's go get your gear and go fishing. Where's your car?"

"Behind the Inn."

"Then come ride with me in my bush car."

"Don't mind if I do," said my smiling Irish railroader with the fairly un-Celtic name of Kushner.

Morris was toting almost as much fishing gear in his big shiny car as I do in my bush car—which is one hell of a lot of gear—including what seemed stacks and stacks of fly rods, from which he selected three—the only time before or since that I've accompanied a man fishing who carried so many rods on a one-day trip.

We headed for a beaver dam up on Deer Creek (the name of which I think I can safely mention since, at last count, I'm sure there are more Deer Creeks in Michigan than ever there were deer). On the way Morris told me he was a retired tool-and-die maker who'd made his bundle by finally forming his own company and making whatever it is master tool-and-die makers make for the big Detroit auto firms—which Morris carefully explained to me but which fell upon the helplessly blocked ears I seem to get in the face of anything faintly technical.

"Where'd you ever pick *that* up?" I wistfully inquired, wondering if there were any cram courses an old fisherman might take in a subject that allowed him to drive a big roomy car full of fishing gear all the way out to Montana.

"Mostly being a helper to men who already knew," Morris explained, adding that he'd been at it virtually since a boy, when his parents brought him over here from Russia.

"Oh," I said, pensively reflecting that tool-and-die making probably wasn't my cup of tea anyway, since I had yet to learn even to tie a decent fly.

When finally we bounced our way into the lovely old dam, Morris nimbly leapt out and rigged up all three fly rods. "Well," I could not help remarking, "I must say you come well prepared, Morris."

"They're all brand-new and I wanted to try them out actually fishing," Morris explained, and once again I wondered why fate had denied me the career of a tool-and-die maker.

Few fish were rising during the heat of the day, but

141

while waiting for Morris to assemble his bamboo arsenal
I spotted a nice riser on the far side and pointed it out to
him.

"Why don't you try for him while you're waiting?"
Morris suggested.

"Too big a deal to cross over," I said.

"I mean try from this side."

"Thanks, chum," I said, "but I'd be lucky to lay out a
decent fly half that distance."

"Then I'll try," Morris said, unhooking a fly from a
set-up rod and quickly working out line and, before my
unbelieving eyes, laying out a superb cast about ten feet
above the steady far riser.

"Lovely, lovely," I murmured.

The fly floated over the fish; the trout rose; and Morris struck.

"Clean missed him," Morris squealed, grinning from
ear to ear, thrusting his new wonder rod out at me.
"Here, you try for him when he starts again."

"No way," I said, shaking my head. "I'd need a sling-
shot ever to cast a fly that far."

"But maybe you can with my rod," Morris insisted. "I
built lots of power into this one."

"*You* did?" I said, puzzled. "You mean you *made* the
rod I'm holding?"

"Of course. Made all three of 'em. In fact, made all the
rods you saw back in my car."

"Oh," I said, a light dawning. "You buy the blanks or
kits or whatever and then assemble them?"

142

"No," Morris said, shaking his head. "I build all my
rods strictly from scratch and I even designed and built
the machine I make 'em with."

"Oh," I said, completely awed, recalling a wobbly wooden stool I'd made in high school that nobody has yet ever quite dared actually sit on. "Oh."

Morris's trout had meanwhile obligingly resumed rising, so with much trepidation I went through the motions of trying to cast a fly over him. I succeeded, of course, or I wouldn't be telling the story now, doing it with more ease in fact than I usually cast half the distance. The whole thing so stunned me that when the trout quickly rose and took I reared back in amazement and cost Morris a favorite fly.

"Wowie!" I hollered. "That's gotta be the longest cast I ever made." I hesitated, groping for the right words. "Morris," I finally ventured, "do you make rods like this —er—professionally?"

"You mean do I make 'em to sell?"

"Well, yes."

"No," Morris said, grinning. "I only make 'em because I love to make nice things for myself and my friends."

"Oh," I said, crushed.

"And since we're now old friends and you've found a rod of mine you like, keep it, my friend. It's all yours."

"Oh," I said faintly, torn between hugging my lovely new rod and the generous artist who made it.

This took place, I'd guess, about five or six years ago. For several summers after that Morris would stop off on his way to more distant fishing climes to spend a day or so fishing. And, despite my feeble protestations, never once did he leave without leaving behind still another magic Kushner rod in which he'd mingled both his genius and his love.

143

The last time I saw Morris he was accompanied by his wife, Fannie, a warm-hearted, attractive, and friendly woman who blushed like a girl when Morris insisted over dinner on telling me how he had courted her during their early Detroit days by taking her out riding on his very first motor vehicle—a brand-new Harley-Davidson motorcycle.

Then, about two summers ago, came my last letter from Morris saying he didn't think he could make it up my way that season. "The old Harley is clunking on about half a cylinder," he wrote, "and just may be running out of gas." Even more depressing were the implications of his scribbled postscript saying he'd decided to sell all his rods.

That was in June and my fears were not groundless. The following month I got a thoughtful letter from his son Victor that his father had passed away. Since then I've heard from another son, Seymour, which so eloquently confirms my suspicion that fly rods are best built for love rather than for money that I'd like to quote from it.

"It is my opinion," he wrote, "that the reason my dad's rods are so excellent is that he was a master craftsman and built them with endless care in an effort to achieve his dream of perfection.

"The machine he built was ingenious and his own creation, but still it was only a milling machine. Just as all violin makers use chisels, gouges, and saws, yet not all violins are comparable in quality . . . His fly rods were truly a labor of love."

I still have and treasure my Kushner rods, of course, and sometimes it seems when I use one of them I see out yonder over the water the smiling smoke-wreathed face of the immensely gifted Russian-Jewish genius whom I once mistook for a retired Irish railroader.

14 Women Fishermen: Are They for Real?

While I suppose it would be monstrously morbid for an old fisherman to keep brooding about such a thing—not to mention being a shocking revelation of piscatorial obsession—I must confess that of late years it has occasionally swept over me that I must in my fashion have devoted more time to fishing than many fairly adult adults ever manage to live. Equally shocking is the accompanying realization that during all that time I don't think I've encountered more than a handful of women anglers on the stream. This seems so incredible, even as I write it, that perhaps I'd better explain what I mean, possibly narrowing the field rapidly by first explaining what I don't mean.

First of all, I don't mean the women anglers I've gone fishing with, though they too have been remarkably few, for the rather obvious reason that the very fact they were accompanied at once removes them from the narrow field of those I started talking about. Nor do I mean what one might call those designing lady anglers whose apparent passion for

the sport is but part of a larger design, involving a powerful love potion called propinquity, for hooking an un-
wary male. Nor those lonely ladies who sometimes travel
in groups and find themselves uneasily embarked on
fishing cruises, all the while ever so wistfully hoping to
land almost anything but a goddam fish. Nor those ex-
pensively clad dames who waggle their three-hundred-
dollar rods in dainty synchronism with their patrician
fannies as they practice for their next casting lesson with
that cute bronzed instructor.

Lastly, I don't mean what is probably the most prev-
alent type of miscalled lady angler—those leisured ladies
who annually haunt our more watery summer resorts
and whose periodic sashays at fishing are but part of a
carefully ritualized gay summer whirl that includes
sailing, swimming, sunning, shopping, snoozing, shuf-
fleboarding (damn, I'm running out of esses!), golfing,
riding, tennis, bridge, beauty doctoring, cocktail hour-
ing, dining, dancing—all occasionally seasoned by a
discreet pinch of flirting . . .

In other words I don't mean those so-called women
fishermen who (like so many of their male counterparts,
for that matter) only play and posture at fishing, who fish
more for status than for fish, and who often as not
secretly regard it as one of the more boring of all the odd
things one must do to keep getting invited to all the right
places by all the right people.

No, the rare kind of woman fisherman I mean is a far
different breed—a lone, perspiring, hair straggling,
mosquito-haloed creature wading up to her whizzle
string in rough water, all the while casting like crazy and
wearing a beatific expression that proclaims to the world

147

what a ball she's having and all but shouting pee on society . . .

As much as I've ever thought about it I guess I absently concluded, in a sort of smug Victorian fog, that fishing simply wasn't a woman's bag; that inherent feminine fear and innate daintiness naturally made them avoid the brambles; and, anyway, what real *lady* would ever want to hobnob out there with all those toads and snakes and grunting bears? In other words, I guess I ever so comfortably concluded that my kind of fishing was not only never meant for women but was, like stag movies, divinely created for us males alone and in fact came bursting upon our masculine world bearing Jehovah's own official stamp "For Men Only."

Even the most fleeting reflection pretty well stamps all this as a lot of emulsified hogwash. Surely any heroic soul who can bring herself to contemplate, much less face, having a time bomb planted in her belly and toting it around for months ticking and swelling and then having it wrenched from her can face any terrors one can conjure up on any trout stream—including a herd of stampeding elephants. No, there's simply got to be some other reason for the absence of women on our backbush trout waters, and the more I think about it the more I suspect it is us bloody men.

Now it is not my purpose here to assess blame or point the accusing finger of guilt at any gender but rather to explore ever so detachedly how come the gals are missing all the fishing fun. So to launch things gently I'll begin by venturing the guess that the main reason women don't fish more is that we men don't want them out there and, moreover, have spent one hell of a lot of time and talent

148

keeping them away. This we've accomplished in many ways and, though my sequences may be shaky, I'll further venture to name a few.

First, for countless generations in almost every society and clime men have fostered the legend that it is most unladylike when not outright indecent for any woman to aspire to do that which men prefer to do alone. And hunting and fishing have long traditionally teetered on top of the male totem vying for first place among all the many things men have ordained verboten to women. Let's face it, for more years than even history can recall both fishing and hunting have been exclusive masculine clubs with large neon signs blazing over the stout pad-locked front doors reading "No dogs or women allowed!" (In many hunting clubs, of course, certain select breeds of dogs are seasonably reprieved along with an occasional cleaning lady.)

Nature has both conspired and been used in bringing about this tidy state of affairs. Manly little boys have long been expected and indeed trained to bang-bang their way into manhood just as nice little girls are fully ex-pected—from the moment they put down their last dollies and take up boys—to start having a procession of real live dollies all their own—unselfishly abetted (or should I say a-bedded?) between fishing trips by us per-petually amorous males—the care and feeding of which leaves them precious little time ever to learn how to fish or to do so had they learned.

The formula runs in a monotonous circle, repetitive as a broken record: a guy hates to take his gal fishing because she doesn't know how and instead just sulks in the car swatting mosquitoes and running down the bat-

149

tery honking the horn or listening to the soaps and panting to leave, all of which, sensitive soul that he is, tends to upset his fishing; the gal never learned to fish because no guy ever took her; so a guy hates to take his gal fishing because . . .

In other words, during that brief period when she might have had a little time to learn and form a taste for fishing nobody bothered to take her; and when next, after a gap of umpteen years, she again has the leisure to learn and actually go fishing it's either too damn late or she discovers that meanwhile she's grown to loathe the whole cotton-pickin' business.

This last suggests one of the more subtle gambits we men have long used to keep our private hunting and fishing preserves to ourselves: making the women envy and come finally to hate the things we especially cherish. Look (though I may rue the day I ever put this in writing), fishing must be just about the most selfish, egotistical, time-consuming, self-absorbing (not to *mention* expensive) pastime in all the world—and the women bloody well know it. So naturally, if the poor neglected souls can't join in this fascinating thing that keeps forever luring their menfolks away for so many hours and days, they're going to wind up hating it.

My mother-in-law's only daughter once put the female lament with brevity and eloquence. "If you were out chasing blondes I might be able to do something about it," she wailed, "but tell me, oh tell me if you can and dare, how any mere woman can compete with a fish!"

There are probably many other reasons why women don't get to fish like men, but whatever they are and granting mine are all wrong, there is one thing I'm dead

150

sure of: it's *not* because women can't learn how to fish and grow to love it as much as any man. One reason I'm so sure of this is my long-held conviction that despite all the esoteric nonsense spun about the art, any person who possesses sufficient coordination to tie his own shoelaces can learn to cast a decent fly; another is that I've known and fished with a number of women fishermen I'd stack against any guys I know. Indeed, I think I'll wind up this belated confessional by saluting a few of these happy rebels who by their emancipation have figuratively told us lordly males to go flour our balls and chains.

FRANK STEEL'S DAUGHTER

I guess I'll have to refer to her simply as Frank Steel's daughter, though I'm sure her first name is hidden somewhere in the fading old fishing notes I've compulsively kept for nearly forty years listing every fishing trip I've ever taken and who I fished with, besides recording the catch (or lack of it), the weather, the state of my hangover, and other deathless fishing data. So if she should ever read this I do hope she'll forgive me, because lately I find it too depressing to paw through my old notes and keep running into the names of old fishing pals (including Frank himself, alas) who now do their fishing beside still waters in distant celestial meadows I can't seem to find on any maps . . .

Anyway, notes or no notes, Frank Steel's daughter was, I'm pretty sure, just about the first really top-notch woman angler I ever fished with, though she was then but a girl in her late teens, I'd guess. Of course she had several things going for her, including a teacher (her

151

father, Frank) who then held the unique distinction (and still may for all I know) of being the only fisherman around to hold *two* world's records: one for dry-fly casting and the other for catching the largest chinook salmon.

How I (who have never won even a local door prize) ever happened to be fishing in such unlikely fast company came about this way. My old chum Wells Watkins of Chicago was and is a charter member of the Michigan Northwoods Club near here. Years ago we somehow met, probably out fishing (again, my scary old notes would doubtless reveal all, but . . .), and we hit it off. So when one summer he invited his old friend Frank Steel up for fishing, Frank and I naturally met and Frank became instantly intrigued with the wild brook trout fishing I showed him. So when during still another summer Wells invited both Frank and his daughter up I naturally took them out to a remarkable stretch of wadable river that harbored (and still harbors, hence my not naming it) some glorious, hard-to-catch wild trout.

Though I may have forgotten Frank's daughter's first name I'll never forget her fishing. At the first splashing rise she let out a squeal and piled into the fast water and proceeded to fish rings around both of us. Now this is no big feat as far as I am concerned, I'll ruefully admit, but to behold a mere slip of a girl beating the pants off a *double* world's champ . . . When the day was far spent, Frank and I had virtually to lasso her to get her off the misting stream and rush her off to the old Midway to feast on those glorious barbecued spareribs they used to serve. So, wherever she is, I salute the first woman fisherman who opened my eyes to the hitherto unsus-

152

pected possibility that the world of "good" fishermen knows no gender.

Since the writing of the foregoing Wells Watkins answered my recent letter of inquiry and revealed that the girl's name is Carol and further that she later went on to become the women's national fly-casting champion. So for once, at least, I managed to spot a winner! Wells's thoughtful letter continues, "Frank Steel's 83-pound chinook held the world's record for thirty or forty years but it was broken, I believe, some four years ago. He was also the first man to make a perfect score of 100 in a dry-fly casting tournament, in which competition he became a national champion, as well as in the wet fly and skish. Frank died about ten years ago."

DOTSIE

Dotsie Shoemaker was one of the few women I ever bothered to help learn to fly-fish, I'm ashamed to admit, and if she didn't go on to win any national prizes, in my book she became before she left here one of the most enthusiastic and indefatigable fly-fishermen I've ever known.

One of my most vivid memories of the effervescent Dotsie was the day we slugged our way into a remote deep cranberry-bogged headwaters pond and launched *two* boats—the only moderately sane way ever to dare fish it unless from a balloon. I'd had fabled luck there on several previous trips catching and busting off on big deep-chested wild brooks, but *this* day, as so often happens when one fisherman dares show another a really special spot, we couldn't catch even a lily pad, though we flailed away for hours.

When, almost gratefully, I finally heard an ominous roll of thunder and wheeled to see a glowering sky bearing down on us like a wayward bus, I relievedly suggested a hasty retreat.

"Better we get going, Dotsie," I suavely purred, paddling away for the one safe landing spot, "or you'll get soaked and imperil your three-dollar permanent."

"Just a few more casts," Dotsie begged, not even looking away. "You go on ahead, fraidy cat."

Since I've never relished fishing or indeed been able to fish in thunderstorms, I shrugged and landed and dragged my rubber tub up to the bush car and had barely finished lashing it on when the storm broke.

"Dotsie!" I wailed out the dripping car window amidst the wildly forking shafts of lightning and awesome booms of thunder that seemed to shake the ground.

"Coming soon," I heard a distant voice calling.

Meanwhile the storm raged on as I huddled in the bepelted car, wincing my eyes shut with each new jagged lightning bolt but grateful I'd somehow survived to hear the booming response, listening tensely to the crackling and crashing all around me, sounding for all the world like a giant forest fire in a gale, dismally wondering how poor drenched Dotsie was ever making it. Presently the fireworks subsided enough so I could reel down a window and let out another despairing yelp.

"Daw-oat-seee!" I wailed like a banshee.

"Here I am!" I heard a voice shouting and then the other car door flew open and I wheeled to behold a dripping and woefully bedraggled but triumphant Dot-

155

sie thrusting a glorious and still-wriggling brook trout under my nose. "Aren't you proud of your latest pupil, Izaak Walton?" she crooned.

"Yes, but get in, get in," I said petulantly, starting up the motor, "after you've subdued that bloody fish, that is, and before it swims away."

"But the boat, the boat?" Dotsie said, waving her wriggling fish. "Aren't we going to wait out the storm and go get it?"

"I'll leave that till my next trip," I said, racing the motor. "Moreover, if we go back down there I just know you'll want to crawl right back in it and go fishing."

"Fraidy cat," Dotsie said, reluctantly crawling into the car hugging her dripping prize.

INGRID

Here I must throw a slight curve and confess at the outset that I've never yet fished with Ingrid Bartelli, the main reason being that I'm scared stiff to tackle the favorite trout water of both herself and her husband, Len: a wild, mountain-girded, swirling, down-logged stretch of the upper Yellow Dog that gives me mental hernia even to think of wading. Yet if she fishes with half the zeal and savvy she brings to our wild-mushroom hunts (of which her knowledge is simply awesome), I just know she's got to be a fishing whiz.

Ingrid belongs here anyway because of her deep love of the outdoors and all its lore. Before I got to know her I rather fancied myself as a fairly savvy amateur naturalist, but after a few trips with Lady Ingrid I knew I'd been groping my way through the woods sightless ever since boyhood. She can rattle off the names, both popular and Latin, of all manner of shrubs and herbs and wild flowers and vines and trees and mosses and various fungi, including mushrooms, of course, like the kids today can tick off the ten top tunes. In fact, if I were king the first thing I'd do would be to appoint Ingrid the leader of all future field trips for *both* the Boy and Girl Scouts of America. She loves nature and knows nature and moreover can tell what she feels and knows, a rare combination in our heedless times. Meanwhile, I'm checking over my accident policies in preparation for our next summer's safari together on her favorite stretch of the upper Yellow Dog. If *she* can dare fish it, certainly *I* can in this new age of dawning rapport between Hisn and Hernia . . .

QUEEN MARTHA MARIE

I first met Paul Young's widow, Martha, when she presided over the busy Detroit sporting goods store she and her rod-building husband then still ran. By that time Paul had pretty well given up his own fishing because of the heart condition that finally carried him off, and when I'd drop by Paul and I would usually retreat to his lofty back room amidst all the mysterious lathes and precious racks of tonkin cane and naturally talk about—what else? —fishing.

Rarely did Paul fail to inquire about his favorite Driggs River (an Upper Peninsula stream I had to drive across to reach sylvan Detroit), which he once so loved to fish and for which he named one of his own lovely bamboo creations. I still have several rods made by Paul himself (now

157

prized collectors' items), including one real oldie Paul used himself, a weepy old Thomas that used to make me feel like Nijinsky himself when I'd get waving it with a full head of line. But to get back to Martha Marie . . .

It was only after Paul died that I got to know Martha better, for the first time learning that she herself was an avid fisherman, as I might all along have suspected. As our friendship grew, mostly by mail (since I'd cagily send my orders directly to her), a few summers ago I timidly ventured to invite her to come fishing up my way and bring a chum. Much to my amazement I got a note back saying she'd arrive the following week with her old friend and fishing pal Rosalynde Johnston — a decision doubtless measurably assisted less by the prospect of my dazzling piscatorial company than the unseasonable low water then prevailing on their favorite AuSable — where both had and have cabins and Rosalynde now lives year round.

Anyway, the two ladies arrived and I somehow made room for them and their gear in my jam-packed bush car (really an ambulant summer home) and whirled them off to a remote and spectacularly beautiful stretch on the lower Yellow Dog, where I once fished regularly for spunky wild brooks before I was so hopelessly bitten by the bug of haunting quiet waters. On the way there I spun such glowing tales of all the fishing goodies that lay ahead that the ladies understandably worked themselves into a genteel lather of expectation.

"Here we are," I said, slamming on the brakes halfway down a steep cliffside sand hill. "Here's where we rig up."

"But where's the water?" Rosalynde inquired.

"Com wit ol' Pierre zee guide," I beckoned the ladies, and we took a few steps and peered down, and there far below us saw a thin, glittering strip of quicksilver flashing and dancing its way between narrow aisles of towering pines. "That's where we'll fish," I said, pointing. "And I'm sure it will amaze you."

Amazed all of us indeed were when shortly we discovered we had reckoned without the superior piscatorial wisdom of the fisheries soothsayers in Lansing who, with the detached omniscience evidently afforded by distance alone, had recently decreed that a cold, rushing, mountainous, northern torrent that had spawned and supported oceans of wild brook trout ever since the last glacier suddenly panted for nothing but the immediate planting of several bargeloads of house-broken hatchery-raised browns.

The poor lonely little devils were so plentiful I could wade right in among them, as during a sucker run, and as I picked out a fly they came swimming up in schools rolling their eyes up at me for a handout, much like the sad-eyed moochers on North Clark Street. After I'd caught and released perhaps a dozen of these waifish identical twins I abruptly quit, took down my rod, plumped myself on a rock, and so roundly and loudly cursed out the geniuses in Lansing that Martha and Rosalynde came running to the rescue.

"Sorry," I said, widening my hands. "I simply didn't know about this latest officially planned calamity. But I do know a place I swear still has only wild brook trout." I sighed. "At least it did until dusk *yesterday*—that's unless the nocturnal branch of the busy Lansing wrecking crew up and planted a load of tiger sharks there during the night."

"Let's go," the ladies gamely responded, and so we

159

trudged up the sand hill and took down our wands and shortly found ourselves rolling along toward Frenchman's Pond.

There, quite by accident we ran into my old friend L. P. "Busky" Barrett, who'd brought along a couple of steaks on the off chance I'd show up at what was one of our shared favorite spots. So when the greetings were over Busky and I sat and inhaled a few indiscreet sips of bourbon and watched the ladies rig up and proceed to put on a superb exhibition of quiet trout stalking and controlled casting. We watched them until the sun started curving down and Busky turned to his charcoaling chores, and later that evening we dined in the open, watching the nighthawks wheeling and the trout dimpling, devouring Busky's steaks after a dreamy preliminary course of freshly caught wild brook trout, compliments of the ladies.

Martha recently wrote me and filled me in on some routine questions I'd asked her (How long have you been fishing, etc., etc.?), and I find her answers so beguiling I can't resist quoting much of her reply.

"When I was very young in France I used to fish with my father, but I really didn't learn to fly-fish until I met Paul. I was then seventeen and still going to school, but we used to skip school and go fish those wonderful streams just outside Duluth. From then on it was fly-fishing every chance we could. When our boys were little tots we would take them along, and when Paul had a fish on he'd let Jack reel it in while sitting on Paul's shoulders. In Detroit the streams were farther away, but when we lacked a car we simply rode the streetcars till we found some sort of fishing. Paul and I fished in many states, always together, and he didn't mind telling people I'd often catch more fish than he.

"You ask about my most memorable fishing trip. Surely one such was the time years ago when Paul guided me to a special spot on the Boardman during the height of the July caddis hatch, my first experience with this spectacular hatch. Anyway, Paul told me to wait there and then took off for a nearby beaver dam. So I waited and waited until I doubted there was a fish in the river. Then the hatch broke, and soon it seemed millions of flies were soaring overhead, zooming and whirring like tiny airplanes. Then as the flies started settling the fish started rising, and honest to goodness, I never saw or likely will ever see a river so come to life. I kept casting and casting but didn't quite know about the striking you have to do in a caddis hatch, so in despair I almost tried to net them, they were flopping so close. Finally, I figured I'd better strike every time I saw any kind of rise near my fly, and this strategy worked, and before long I'd caught a 16-incher and then an 18-incher, and then my biggest prize of all, a 23-inch brown. When finally I got him in the net I just hugged it and made for shore, and I still have it mounted skin style at my cabin on the AuSable. Paul soon came back, empty handed, and if only he'd stayed where he'd planted me he would really have had the finest fishing of our career."

The longer I fish the less I know what makes up a "good" fisherman, it combines so many things; technique being but a part of it. But whatever it takes, Martha Marie somewhere received the full charge. Now superla-

161

tives have little place in fishing, I've always felt, but Martha disarms the usual restraints, so today I'll shoot the works and proclaim that Martha Marie Young is not only the best woman fly-fisherman I've ever known (no great compliment, since they've been so relatively few), but one of the very best top fly-fishermen of any gender I've ever known or fished with—and *that's* been a staggering crew. And real class seems to attract real class, at least in fishing, for I must add that her dear friend and fishing pal Rosalynde Johnston isn't far behind her royal highness, Queen Martha Marie herself.

P.S. to Gloria and Germaine: When you gals come up to pin on my medal you'll find me out fishing at Frenchman's.

15 *The Dancing Fly*

1

My name is Al and I'm here to tell my fellow anglers—
wups!—and all those dear lady anglers, too (if the former will please kindly forgive this old bourbon bibber his
sly women's libber bow to the latter), that Frenchman's
Pond is by all odds the most fascinating and frustrating
trout water I have ever fished—and I've been angling
like crazy since before I could spell it.

Fascinating I find Frenchman's because I am one of
the few fishermen in these parts who happens to know
that the place is simply crawling with lovely wild trout
(most fishermen not even knowing of the pond's existence); frustrating because my pals and I can't catch
them—with sufficient regularity, that is, to avoid the
sneaking suspicion that on those rare occasions when we
do catch a few it isn't all blind luck. Frenchman's Pond, in
other words, gives graduate courses
in fisherman's humility on almost
any old day a guy dares visit it. Tui-
tion-free courses.

My old fishing buddies Timmy
and Pinky share my views about the
pixilated place and in fact we three

163

were together the first time ever we laid eyes on it. This memorable visit occurred last summer on a warm evening in mid-June when we slugged our way in there on foot, all on a hunch of little Timmy's, who is forever collecting and poring over tattered old maps in the hope of discovering some remote and overlooked trout Shangri-La.

Our first trip in was one prolonged fight—fighting brush, fighting clouds of fisherman-starved insects, fighting hidden sump holes in the swampy stretches we had to hack our way through. Our leader, little Timmy, disdained using a compass and instead led us over a tortuous and indistinct old tote road which he was positive would lead us straight to our latest trout paradise only because his latest antique map said it would.

About the time a puffing Pinky and I were about ready to conclude that Timmy's ancient cartographer was taken drunk the day he drew his map, Timmy stopped and held his finger to his lips and whispered "Listen!" We gratefully stopped and listened and, sure enough, heard the shrill, insistent cries of what must have been a million frogs, sounding at first for all the world like an army of vying youngsters blowing toy whistles at the tops of their lungs.

"Can't be far," Timmy whispered, pushing on and again, sure enough, we hadn't gone fifty paces when our road ended abruptly on a granite bluff overlooking a lonely and desolate expanse of water. Our presence disturbed a pair of blue herons below and they rose with great comic commotion, threshing extravagantly for altitude, and then, with all the languor of a slow-motion movie, flapped silently away on oiled wings.

"See!" Timmy announced triumphantly, complacently folding his map away and patting it. "Old tote road ends exactly where old map says it should. How about that?"

"First there was Magellan the Magnificent," I intoned, "followed by Timmy the Intrepid."

"Look, fellas!" Pinky suddenly croaked, pointing bug-eyed at the pond below. *"Look what I see!"*

Timmy and I looked—and saw unfolding on the water below us the wildest rise of trout any of us had ever beheld. As far as the eye could see, scores of trout were dimpling and sending out widening magic rings, and for a moment I had the illusion we'd been caught in a freak hailstorm. But no, for in their eagerness some of these trout were leaping clear out of water — just like on the outdoor magazine covers—and landing with a smack we could hear on our bluff.

For a long time we stood there, still panting and perspiring from our trek, watching the crazy piscatorial fireworks. Yet even as we gaped I felt the first small premonition that this place just might not yield its trout gladly—an intuition we ever so richly had confirmed.

First of all, I could see at a glance that Frenchman's Pond wasn't truly a pond at all—Timmy's treasured old map to the contrary—but rather the long narrow meandering backwater of an old inactive beaver dam originally built on a flowing stream. Down on our left we could see the faint brush-covered outline of the old dam itself, while the serpentine backwater seemed roughly to follow the wavering contour of the granite range on which we stood. Another clue that the fishing mightn't be easy—at least from shore—was that the pond was heavily forested mostly by tall spruces to the very waterline on the far side while on our side, though fairly open,

165

it was boggy-margined clear back to our granite range, with ominous patches of open water showing through— sometimes a real quick way, I ruefully knew, for a careless fisherman to disappear abruptly and maybe not emerge until weeks later in droll places like Singapore.

"Looks sorta kinda like tough fishing," Timmy said, reading my thoughts.

"We might try dapping flies from a balloon," Pinky suggested helpfully. "If only we'd brought a balloon."

All of us were sufficiently battle-scarred veterans of past collisions with old beaver dams to suspect that the water would also probably be shallow (thus making these spooky wild trout all the more scary) as well as unwadable from the long accumulation of silt. Meanwhile the frogs kept up their shrill clamor and the trout their steady feeding so we banished our suspicions and rigged up with trembling hands.

"Looks like Frenchman's got us hooked," Timmy murmured prophetically as, our bamboo wands assembled, we slid our way down the steep hill on an old deer trail to join the fray.

Once out on the wobbly bog we quickly separated, as fishermen do, Pinky taking up his stand on the wide watery margin and immediately uncorking and starting to flail away. Timmy shrugged and headed upstream and I nodded and hooked my thumb and headed for the old beaver dam below, fishing as I went.

Soon we lost sight of each other and as I staggered and reeled my way along, occasionally pausing and balancing myself enough to paste out a fly, I felt less like a fisherman than a gesticulating drunk on a trampoline. Keeping in character I presently contrived to step in a hidden

166

bog hole, sinking well over one hip boot. After I'd wallowed my way out, holding my rod high like an Olympic torch and still gasping from the shock, it quickly swept over me that among its other allurements the waters of Frenchman's were colder than the deepfreezes of hell.

Hours later we met back up on the bluff, chilled to the bone, our hands shaking so much that our wavering flashlights looked more like blinking fireflies.

"Confess!" Timmy said, his breath emerging in thin vaporous jets. "I didn't catch a bloody fish or get a bloody pass."

"Me too," Pinky confessed.

"That makes us even," I said, cupping my ear. "And you can still hear 'em flopping down there." We listened, and sure enough, even above the din of the frogs, mixed now with the shrill cries of nighthawks feeding overhead, we could hear the steady *slurp-slurp* of the still-feeding trout.

"Frenchman's may have us hooked," Pinky remarked as we came to the first swamp, "but we sure in hell haven't its trout."

"There's gotta be a way," little Timmy murmured, plunging into a maze of tag alders.

The next evening we were back again at Frenchman's, of course, and the next evening after that. But the verdict remained the same: still no trout and no offers.

"At least we're hacking out a pretty fair hiking trail," Pinky said. "For water buffalo, that is."

So excited were we over the pristine fishing we'd found if not solved at Frenchman's that we decided not to risk reopening the old tote road so that we might drive

167

our bush car in. For if we could drive in, so might curious rival fishermen, we figured, and if they did pretty soon our precious pond would inevitably land on the tourist beat, complete with ambulant septic toilets. This prospect so scared us we took to hiding our parked car, the better to cover our tracks, as well as leaving the first quarter mile or so of the old tote road in the tangled state we found it so that no prying hardier souls might be tempted to hike in and so spread the word.

Our strategy worked and no fishermen bothered us, but the hell of it still was that neither did the trout. This virtually fishless state of affairs ran on so long that first summer that finally we limited our visits strictly to weekends. This we did not simply to solace our tattered pride but to preserve also at least a smidgin of domestic tranquillity. After all, if three braggy fishermen couldn't occasionally bring home at least one wizened trout, mightn't the home front naturally begin wondering what other dark shenanigans we might be up to?

"Anyway, we mustn't be too greedy," Pinky said. "Seven pratfalls a week is too much for any gentleman angler."

Despite all our frustrations at Frenchman's we naturally learned more about the place as the summer wore on, including gathering more clues to help solve the baffling enigma of why its trout were so reluctant to commit suicide with any degree of regularity. Two of our biggest finds came the day we toted in our inflatable wading floats and swiftly confirmed our suspicions that the water was generally too shallow and the silt too thick to use them for fishing.

168

But this day was devoted to exploring, we told ourselves, and so, eyes glowing with scientific zeal, we had not even uncased our rods. Instead we sweatily persisted, kicking and churning our way through spreading clouds of silt like a marauding trio of ink-ejecting squid. From our exhausting labors we learned two things we felt helped mightily to explain our astonishing run of fishing disasters.

First we found the place abounding with easily accessible natural food, principally hordes of minnows and scads of tiny freshwater shrimp burrowed in the silt. Our next benumbing eye-opener—in more ways than one— was the further discovery that the water in Frenchman's was incredibly cold—I'd had a taste of it on that first day —in turn doubtless accounted for by the fact that for its entire winding length the place abounded with scores of bubbling underwater springs, both large and small. Timmy, our acknowledged intellectual, quickly enlightened us on the ominous consequences often attending such a combination.

"All this easy grub makes it all the more easy for the trout to ignore our flies," he declaimed as we shivered and danced around an open fire on our cliff top while thawing out. "At the same time, this frigid water naturally sharply lowers their metabolism—"

"I was a kindergarten dropout, p- p- pal," shivering Pinky broke in. "What's this here now fancy m- m-metabolism?"

"Means the little bastards never get so goddam hungry, stupid."

"Sorry, Herr Doktor. P- please proceed."

"Which in turn means," Timmy concluded, "that naturally our poor little fake flies don't even have the usual Chinaman's chance to attract them." He widened his hands. "It's as simple as that."

169

"One thing puzzles me, Timmy," I said, putting in my oar. "Granting all you say, why is it these presumably anemic and easily gorged trout at Frenchman's continue to spurn our flies and yet hit the naturals here like crazy?"

"Beats me too," Timmy admitted, wagging his head. "All of which puts a finger smack on the big problem we gotta solve." All of which in turn brings me smack down to the most baffling enigma of all at Frenchman's.

For good old Frenchman's — as if all its other afflictions weren't enough to drive us screaming from the place—had one final trick up its sleeve calculated to preserve its trout and sap our waning sanity: its fly hatches were like no other fly hatches any of us had ever seen. Instead of the widely varied and predictable succession of aquatic insects that occurs annually on most trout waters all season long, year in and year out, only one species of fly kept hatching over and over on Frenchman's, or so it seemed. Not only that but this unique Frenchman's fly was almost too tiny to be seen by the naked eye and moreover it looked more like an animated ball of fur than a fly. Finally, to top things off, the damned thing danced — ah yes — forever it crazily danced and danced, up and down, up and down. In fact, in a sunburst of creativity we immediately christened it the Dancing Fly.

While none of us was really up on our entomology or, for that matter, a more than passably savvy amateur bug man, all of us had seen midge flies before, of course, and even carried a small emergency assortment of "bought-en" imitations in our boxes—all of which the trout at Frenchman's disdainfully ignored.

170

So stubborn Timmy, by far the best tyer among us, reassaulted the pond in a wading float (we now kept one cached there) and gathered up specimens of the Dancing Fly in a bottle and took them home to tie up some imitations. Two days later we tried them out, but either Timmy's hooks were too big or Piscator had a bellyache that day or something went haywire—for they too were spurned like all our other offerings.

"I'll order some smaller hooks first thing tomorrow," Timmy promised grimly as we plodded fishless back out to the car. "Air mail."

"If they get much smaller I'll have to hire a small boy to tie them on for me," Pinky said, squinting wryly.

We wound up that first season at Frenchman's, of course, valiantly trying out Timmy's latest midges, this time tied on the smallest hooks he could find.

"The man wrote they don't make eyed hooks much smaller," Timmy explained as we rigged up for the final assault of the season. Box score: Timmy got cleaned out overstriking a dandy; Pinky got one feeble pass; while I, virtuously shunning the obvious rhyme, fell quietly on my can.

"Damned funny thing," I said as we dragged ourselves out to the car. "While I'm no Art Flick, I'd swear your flies were almost exact imitations of the Dancing Fly, Timmy."

"Scarcely, but thanks anyway for the compliment, pal," Timmy said, modestly fluttering his eyelashes. "But even supposing we *could* tie an exact imitation of the little devils, tell me, how the hell we ever gonna make 'em dance?"

171

2

"Look, fellas," I announced casually on the first day of fishing the following spring when once again we stood on our granite bluff looking down at our tantalizing pond, "last winter I gave a lot of thought to this baffling Frenchman's place, and while I don't claim to have all the answers, I do have a little suggestion to make before we launch the new season that just might help ease our pain."

"Let's have it," Timmy said, lowering his packsack and listening politely.

"I've got it," Pinky said, slapping his thigh. "This season we're gonna start hitting the bottle *before* we start fishing."

"Let the man talk," Timmy said. "Do please reveal your little pain-killing plan, comrade."

"First I want to make it perfectly clear," I ran on, ignoring their titters, "that I don't aim to commercialize our fishing or turn the place into a gambling casino."

"Hear, hear," Pinky said. "Ol' fishing pal shuns gambling hell."

"But I do think my little suggestion might not only help us over some of the balder fishing spots but, who knows, even improve the results."

"Goody, we're gonna plant a troupe of topless mermaids in the place," Pinky broke in, clapping his hands. "Then all we gotta do is lay around all day with binoculars and a six-pack, watchin' 'em cavortin' an' dozin' in the sun." He rolled his eyes. "No shenanigans, of course, 'cause my mother done tole me the best thing to do with a sleeping bag is leave her lay."

"You really shoulda been on television," I said scornfully, " 'Cornball Pinky,' they'd call him, 'King of the Reruns'."

"Will you *please* let the man say his piece," Timmy said, frowning at Pinky. "Though I got a faint inkling we're gonna hear a quaint tinkling involving a swap of the coin of the realm."

"That's *it*, Timmy!" I said, nodding brightly. "You just put your finger on it. My little suggestion is that it might be good fun and also stimulate our fishing if we put a friendly little daily bet on the results."

"Like how small?" Timmy said.

"Oh," I said, shrugging. "Not enough to really hurt anyone but still enough to keep us stirred off our dead butts — something say like five bucks a head to the guy who catches the biggest fish."

"My, my. You mean the winner'd dance outa here waving ten bucks — five each from his two pigeons?"

"The daily winner would get his ten bucks, all right," I agreed, "but it might be fairer and even more stimulating all around if we agreed that the guy with the second biggest fish would at least be rewarded by not losing anything, the last guy paying the full shot."

"I don't quite follow."

"Look, supposing here today Pinky up and caught a twelve-incher—"

"First I'd frow up an' then fall down in a heap," Pinky said, pouching out his cheeks and staggering around drunkenly.

"And you, Timmy, an eleven-incher," I ran on, "and me a ten."

173

"Go on, dreamer."

"Under my plan Pinky would cop the ten bucks, all

right, you'd neither win nor lose a dime, while poor little me'd have to fork over the full ten."

"I get what you mean, all right, but supposin' Pinky caught a mere eight-incher, you a seven, an' me somewhere in between? Isn't ten bucks a pretty elegant reward for catching a trout of a size all of us usually return?"

"I've thought of that, Timmy," I said. "We could solve that by setting a pond minimum of, say, ten inches. No ten-inchers caught, all bets off."

"Fair enough, but supposin' only one guy catches a ten-incher or better? Do the other two each pay five though one catches an eight-incher and the other a seven?"

"It's all what we agree to, Timmy," I said loftily. "Personally I think it'd be fairer and even more fun to say that the only way a nonwinner can save himself five bucks is to at least catch a qualifying trout, even if it's finally nosed out."

"Well I'll be damned," Timmy said, wagging his head. "Did you dream all this up or run across it somewhere?"

"It's all my baby, Timmy," I said. "I thought a lot about Frenchman's last winter and in fact I often *did* dream about it."

"As who didn't?" Timmy murmured, rubbing his chin. "But under your bet wouldn't we still be killing fish we'd otherwise like to return?"

"How do you mean?"

"Like say I catch and creel a qualifying ten-incher on my first cast here today and then, just before quitting time, latch on to a twelve."

"I've thought of that too," I said. "We'd fix that by

174

keeping our qualifiers in live traps — I've got three already on order at Bietila's—until either we catch a bigger fish or the betting hour is over. That way everybody could return all or any of his fish, the winner out of sheer euphoria, the losers in bleak despondency."

"I've gotta drinkin' uncle down in Peoria," Pinky said, "but no kin I know of in this here Euphoria."

"You've also gotta bug up your Emporia," Timmy said scathingly, turning and shooting me a shrewd glance. "Looks like you've thought of just about everything, eh, comrade? Beats me how you ever found time to work last winter."

"I've tried to cover every foreseeable contingency, Timmy," I said, laughing, at the same time feeling myself flushing guiltily over all the things I *wasn't* revealing. "What do you say?"

"I'm on," Timmy said, shrugging and spreading his hands. "Can't think of a lovelier way to go broke or else make an easy buck. What hour is the bet off?"

"That would depend," I said, "on when we arrive, the state of the weather or our hangovers, how long we want to fish — variable things like that to be determined each trip. Since today is warm and pleasant and it's still early, how about our closing the bets at five?" Timmy nodded. "After that a guy can suit himself, either keep on fishing a bit or hit the jug or maybe even take a nap." I turned to Pinky. "How about you, lucky?"

"Why not?" Pinky said, nodding. "It'd be worth five bucks just to see a decent trout caught outa this haunted place — though the Lord knows they're here. When do we start?"

175

"Minute we're rigged up," I said, unscrewing my rod

case. "Oh — just one more thing — how about our also agreeing that any day a guy doesn't feel up to betting, all he need do is simply say so—naturally, before making his first cast."

"Natch," Timmy said, shooting me another searching look. "Nice little escape hatch, eh, comrade, just in case your busy little brain failed to think of everything?"

"Fair to everyone," I said virtuously, finally rigged up and heading down the hill. "See you at five, boys."

"Righto," my two pigeons chorused and again I felt myself flushing as I slithered down the hill.

Shrewd little Timmy had been righter than he knew in guessing that I'd thought of just about everything, I mused to myself as I bounced my way along toward the dam. But the poor man really didn't know the half of it, I guiltily reflected, because in all truth I had devoted far more time and thought to solving the problem of the Dancing Fly before ever I dared think of broaching such a risky bet to the fast fishing company I kept.

As I inched my way along the trembling bog avoiding water traps, I reviewed some of the high spots of my busy winter. The first important decision I had made, I recalled, was the uncharacteristically modest one that I was probably not good enough either as a fisherman or fly tyer ever to solve the problem on my own — I'd simply have to seek help from someone. But who? I pondered —or maybe I should better have pondered whom! True, there were a number of first-rate fly tyers in my bailiwick, most of whom I knew, but I also knew that all of them were avid fishermen. And I felt in my bones that any local tyer smart enough to solve the problem of the

Dancing Fly would likely also be smart enough to track down where the little devils danced. No, it was plain I needed outside help.

It was then the inspiration hit me to avoid the obvious approach—such as combing the outdoor magazines and popular fishing books and the like—and instead visit the library of a nearby college. There I was shortly poring over a whole raft of technical articles and books devoted to the esoteric subject of freshwater aquatic entomology. This I did not to seek enlightenment by actually *reading* the baffling material I'd dug up, heaven knows, but only to find one solitary clue identifying one single author who also both fished and tied his own flies.

It was almost Valentine's Day before I'd tracked down such a gifted soul—a teacher in a happily remote northern New England college—following which I *did* read his article, some of which I even faintly grasped. Next I wrote him a glowing fan letter, naturally telling him all about Frenchman's Pond, of course, and especially about the riddle of the Dancing Fly. Finally I pensively wondered whether he might possibly be able to identify the fly from my crude description and, if so, wondered ever so wistfully whether he might not be prevailed upon to tie up some working imitations, cost of course being no consideration . . .

I so fancied the light air of fishing camaraderie in my closing paragraph I even learned it by heart. "The elusive trout at Frenchman's all seem to arrive in their watery world sporting framed master's degrees in evasion," I wrote, "so if you can possibly solve the mystery of the Dancing Fly you will not only make one distracted fisherman eternally grateful but also perform the humanitarian act of likely saving him and his two fishing buddies from the booby hatch."

Anyone can plainly see from the foregoing that there was nothing sneaky in what I was doing and that all along I had obviously planned only to delightfully surprise Timmy and Pinky and of course cut them in on any possible solution. It was only after I'd received the good professor's diabolically ingenious flies, along with his revealing letter, that Satan first reared his ugly head and sorely tempted me. Or was it cupidity? In either case, I'd awakened one recent morning with my little betting scheme laid out cold.

By now I'd reached the old beaver dam, which had become my favorite fishing spot in the pond — just as Pinky's was the wide midpond area he had dubbed the "Big Spring" and Timmy's his coveted "Top Log." Moving carefully now lest a sudden jarring step alert the lunkers I knew dwelt there, I moved over to firmer ground, rested my rod, glanced around to make sure I was alone, and then produced my brand-new pruning shears and went to work to the tinkling watery accompaniment of the dam's overflow.

In less than an hour I'd cut out a wide swath of casting lane in the maze of slender alders and willows behind me, during which I heard at least a half-dozen exciting splashes and had wheeled in time to see the out-rolling rings—all in the same magic spot. This spot I'd privately named the "Hot Spot" because, I'd learned the season before, it was not only one of the deepest pools in the pond but also harbored a hidden protective maze of ancient submerged logs under which lurked some of the loveliest wild brook trout I'd ever seen.

Scanning the dam closely I could see no sign of our Dancing Fly or indeed any insect life on or above the surface (not too surprising in view of the earliness of the season), and I speculated that the dramatic splashes I was hearing might be the occasional overleaps of hungry trout charging after foolish minnows strayed too close to lurking danger.

My labors done, I sat down and took a breather before tying a fresh tippet to my leader. Then I unzipped my vest and pulled out my newest fly box and, again glancing furtively, with a tweezers removed and held in my palm a single fly, rapturously admiring it. For this was my talented professor's exciting imitation of the Dancing Fly which, along with his letter, I'd received only the week before.

While he rarely attempted to identify any aquatic insect without first seeing an actual specimen — the good professor wrote — my Dancing Fly was at once so rare and so uniquely distinctive, and my letter to him so revealing (ahem!), that he did not hesitate to identify this one as a certain rare species of midget mayfly (giving me the impressive Latin name and stressing that it shouldn't be confused with common midges, which are *not* mayflies) noted chiefly for its affinity for extremely cold freshwater accompanied by loads of overripe silt—which twin distinctions Frenchman's, of course, possessed just oodles and oodles of.

Other distinctions, he explained, were the insect's unusually long hatching period, sometimes running for weeks; its further posthatching lingering on the water; and, above all, its eccentric, skeetering, up-and-down movement upon the surface. Few "normal" insect species were ever found where my Dancing Fly dwelt, he further

179

explained, because so few of the former could live in such an environment, while the latter couldn't seem to anywhere else.

There was another big splash at the hot spot and so, with trembling hands, I tied on the professor's imitation for the first big test. As I did so I saw in the clear daylight that only superficially did it resemble the real Dancing Fly, having indeed at its center the same darkish furry balled look but lacking the tiny wings. Beyond this wingless center I saw protruding an almost invisible pattern of fine hairy tendrils of a neutral color. These, his letter explained, gave his imitation the buoyancy subtly calculated to make it dance — but only, mind, if I explicitly followed his accompanying directions.

Two fish rolled suddenly at the same hot spot and, my heart pounding, I jumped up and started feeding out line and, after a quick backward glance, prepared to launch the great experiment. Back and forth, back and forth whistled my undulating line, and then, saying a wee prayer, I released my first business cast.

Out, out flew my line with the speed of a dart and then I saw my leader lazily folding forward and, last of all, the professor's Dancing Fly floating down and gently kissing the surface with the shy, tentative grace of a wisp of windblown thistledown.

Nothing happened, as the professor had warned, so, still following directions, I waited a full minute before making any move, listening only to my thumping heart. Then, slowly raising my rod up to about nine o'clock (as the old-time fly-casting directions so quaintly used to put it), I took up the slack between me and my fly. Then, still following directions, I brought my rod tip down sharply, almost slapping the surface, and my line rippled out like a fleeing serpent and, as the serpent gradually disappeared, lo, before my very eyes my fly began merrily to dance, up and down, up and down . . .

"One fly gone and twenty-three to go!" I yelped when, all in one blinding flash, a glorious trout rose and engulfed my fly and I reared back like a goosed shot-putter and—*ping!*—found myself gloriously cleaned out.

3

Shortly after five I found Timmy and Pinky waiting for me on the granite bluff, standing before a little fire, both of them unrigged and champing to leave.

"Hi," I greeted them cheerily. "How's the old luck?"

"Can't you tell by lookin'?" a dejected Timmy said.

"Same old crapola," Pinky said, making a face. "Not really a big rise but slow and steady all day, some of 'em dandies." He widened his hands. "But good ol' Frenchman's, true to tradition, turned us down cold. How about you, smiley?"

"I'll show you," I said, my grin widening, and I found a mossy spot and undid my creel and poured out a small avalanche of glistening trout running from ten to fourteen inches. "Thought I'd keep a few on account of it's the first day and all and, further, I had no live trap," I ran on as they stared and stared at far and away the best catch any of us had yet had at Frenchman's.

"Of course you hadda keep a few," Timmy murmured, still staring and then gesturing, "but tell me, did you do all *this* with that one little Adams you got on?"

"Mostly," I lied steadily. "But the next biggest one

181

there came on one of your own small weighted Mud-
dlers," I ran on, piling on the falsehoods, at the same
time telling myself that after all I'd done nothing more
than my pals could have done on their own with a little
imagination. Moreover, I further moralized, since actual
money now rode on the result, why should such a dedicated free enterpriser as I be expected to share a secret
that might cost him dough?

Pinky made the first move, fumbling in his jumper and
handing over a crisp new bill. "Hope you got change for a
ten," he said.

"Sure thing," I said, making change deftly as a
carnival barker. "As Timmy here said only this morning,
I've tried to think of everything."

"Up your kilts," Timmy said, thrusting a wad of wrin-
kled ones at me along with a piercing glance. "So the little
Adams turned the trick, eh?"

"Sure did," I said, stashing my winnings and gathering
up my fish. "But who knows, maybe tomorrow it'll be
something else," I philosophized. "Part of the challenge
of the place, don't you think?"

"Also its charm," Timmy said, rubbing the stubble on
his chin. "Well at least tomorrow is another challenging
day, so let's get the hell outta here and get some sleep."

"At least the platitudes around here are free," Pinky
murmured as we left.

My luck held miraculously on succeeding days at
Frenchman's. In fact, I kept winning so monotonously
that it got so at quitting time the only question became
not whether I might win but whether one or both of my
pigeons would have to pay. Meanwhile, I wrote the good
professor an ecstatic letter telling him all about my wild

182

success with his fly. In it I also wondered if he might find time to tie up a few more. And since in his earlier letter he had said he never tied commercially, I cagily enclosed a rather handsome contribution (out of my winnings!) to his college library.

That summer, with the aid of my trusty live trap—which I now kept stashed at the dam—I caught far more lovely trout than ever I took home. This spartan self-denial I exercised largely for sporting reasons, of course, but I must confess that one tiny factor might have been that to do otherwise was akin to robbing one's own piggy bank. Meanwhile I was doubly rewarded by feeling insufferably virtuous while my piggy bank ranneth over . . .

Of course, occasionally there were those inevitable days when none of us qualified for the bet, when indeed one found oneself wondering by day's end if the temperamental place still harbored any trout. On such days I usually sorted out my fly boxes or rearranged the unused decoy flies on my drying pad (for the further confusion of Timmy and Pinky, of course) and sometimes even visited my pigeons at their favorite spots—always ostentatiously sporting almost any fly but my secret pet.

One day about mid-June my pals almost caught me flat-footed. I'd just cast out my secret weapon and was about to make it go into its dance when I heard a twig snap behind me, followed by a muffled curse. So quickly, without turning, I whipped in my fly and snipped off and stashed my treasure and was absorbedly tying on a number 18 Jassid when Timmy and Pinky popped up behind me.

"Oh, you guys sure startled me!" I squealed and gig-

183

gled like a girl, elaborately surprised. "Out for a little stroll, boys, or just drop by to spy on the master angler?"

"Little of both," Timmy said, squinting. "What's that you got tied on?"

"Orange-bodied Jassid," I said, showing him.

"Thought I just saw you changing flies," Timmy persisted. "What'd you take off?"

"Same favorite li'l ol' Adams, but it seems to lack its magic touch today," I lied without blushing. "See," I ran on, displaying my sheepskin lapel pad like a convention badge, "it's still drying out. What's up? You boys ready to quit?"

"Still got about an hour to go," Pinky said after shooting back his cuff and consulting his wrist. "Just checking to make sure you weren't being seduced by a nearsighted mermaid. Have any luck?"

"Pretty slow today," I said, shaking my head. "No seduction offers and caught only one barely twelve-incher on the li'l ol' Adams."

"Still got us beat," Pinky said with a sigh. "Neither of us has caught even one regular keeper. We really came to take lessons from the master—that's if the tuition's right."

"Wanna try it here?" I said, knowing they wouldn't, making as though to reel in and generously move aside.

"Hell no, man," proud Timmy growled, moving on upstream. "Just checkin' to see if some lunker trout had mercifully pulled you in, but no such luck."

184   It would be too cruel and too boring to recount all the trout I caught that summer and all the wagers I won. Up until August, in fact, neither Timmy nor Pinky had won

a single bet, incredible as that may seem against such crafty old fishing hands. Indeed on those few occasions when one did catch a qualifier it simply meant double trouble for the other since under our ground rules he then paid the full shot. Modesty compels me simply to say that by the time August rolled around I'd already won the price of a new fly rod and had my eyes covetously glued on some elegant felt soles. Then on the first day of August—"black August" I came to call it—like a bolt out of the blue, calamity struck—*bang, bang*—twice in quick succession.

First I lost *all* my precious Dancing Flies—a zipper had worked open and (while naturally nothing else did) out popped their special box. Second, this seemed to be the signal for twin disaster: overnight, Timmy's and Pinky's own luck soared off into space. The details are too horrifying so I'll spare them, but during the first days of my black August I lost half a dozen double bets in as many days. Three of these melancholy days I spent virtually on my benumbed hands and knees vainly scouring the chilly bog for my lost treasures—and the next three fighting the wretched summer cold I'd caught for my pains.

The following week I had a brief financial reprieve, spending most of it in bed recovering from my cold and cursing my stupidity in failing to cache at least one sample fly safely at home. My main exercise that week consisted in tottering to the phone trying to reach my professor and plead for replacements. "Sorry, but that line is temporarily disconnected," a taped voice of doom kept monotonously parroting. But still I kept trying until a cheery postcard from Canada broke the bad news: my

185

errant professor was off on an extended field and fishing trip there and wished me good health, tight lines, and aloha—whereupon I had a relapse.

4

It was nearly mid-August before I rejoined the boys at Frenchman's, considerably more wan if not wiser, and proudly spurned their offer to call all bets off until I felt a little less rocky.

"Thanks, chums," I said, "but my fragile health may be just the handicap you've needed."

"Your dough," Pinky said, shrugging. "Anyway, we offered, and maybe your luck will turn."

"You haven't won yet," I said, heading downhill and shakily groping my way toward the dam—after checking all zippers. There I tried out some dainty new spiders I'd got hold of locally, and though they danced fairly well, they simply didn't *look* like the Dancing Fly—which of course the smart trout at Frenchman's divined before ever the flies landed.

Pinky was dead right in his intuition that my luck might turn. It did, all right—it steadily turned worse. For the next nine days hand running, although I fished as if my life depended on it, I lost nine straight bets—all of them double. Nothing seemed to work. Though twice I managed to catch decent qualifying trout, both times during the final calibration scene Timmy's and Pinky's challengers nosed mine out. In fact so monotonously did they split my boodle, along with little pieces of my heart —one day Timmy, the next day Pinky—that it looked almost as if they'd planned it that way.

On the tenth day a mounting curiosity, mingled with a

dash of cupidity, overcame my pride, and along about midafternoon I deserted my favorite dam and sashayed upstream to take a look. While I won't quite say I meant to spy on my pals, I did move with extra care, avoiding the more open bog and taking the granite ridge instead, which just happened to have more cover.

My first inkling that something might be afoot was when I peered down looking for Pinky and discovered he was not at his favorite "Big Spring," where he usually remained glued. Shrugging, I pushed on up the ridge to go discreetly visit little Timmy at his favorite "Top Log." When I got there, peeking from behind a protective balsam, I saw little Timmy was there, all right, but, contrary to his usual practice, was fishing from the heavily forested far side, our spare wading float parked on shore beside him.

"My, my," I murmured to myself, noting the tall wall of spruces virtually nudging his back. "How the hell does the man ever make a decent cast?"

Peering closer, I next picked up the missing Pinky standing on the near or bog side, right down below me, also busily fishing Timmy's same coveted area from the opposite side. But ever fishing the same place at the same time from whatever angle was such a startling procedure for any of us, all prickly loners, that on a hunch I refrained from hailing them, as I was momentarily tempted, and instead silently withdrew behind my balsam.

It was well I did because what I next witnessed was the strangest sight I've ever seen out fishing, and I've beheld some quaking dandies: two fishermen, their rods pointed straight out at each other across the intervening seventy-odd feet of open water, like duelists with bam-

187

boo weapons, slowing raising and lowering their rods in rhythmic unison, up and down; faster, ever faster. As I gaped for a resentful instant I thought they were stealing my rippling-line stuff. But no, for as I leaned farther out for a better look I saw that, whatever in hell else they were up to, their two lines seemed most definitely joined.

Just then a gorgeous trout rose and struck savagely at one or the other of their flies, which, I could not tell, and I almost fell off the cliff when, amidst all the wild threshing, I saw *both* fly rods hooped and vibrating from the strain. Retreating quickly behind my tree I froze in my tracks when I heard the following strange dialogue:

"Whose turn to reel in?" Pinky called across to Timmy in a sort of cross between a hoarse whisper and a strangled shout.

"Yours," Timmy hollered back in the same muffled fashion. "I landed the last dandy, remember?"

Then before my incredulous gaze I beheld Pinky reeling in a superb trout while Timmy's reel fairly sang as he busily stripped off line down to the backing. "Good God," I murmured weakly as the truth suddenly dawned: *my pals' leaders were not only joined but they were fishing the very same fly!*

I heard myself sort of moaning when next I saw Pinky coolly land and release at least a twelve-inch dandy, just like that, at the same time hollering, "Whaddya know — another fightin' rascal just busted another hook."

Held now in a fiend's clutch I watched, fascinated, as Pinky tied on a fresh fly, blew on it daintily, and hollered "Ready?"

Timmy nodded and this time Pinky paid out line while Timmy busily reeled in until I saw both lines held taut

189

and a solitary fly dangling from its dropper, poised directly over Timmy's hot spot.

"Say when," Pinky hollered.

"When," Timmy hollered back.

Then, while I watched with glazed eyes, my pals began raising and lowering their rod tips in stately unison, up and down, up and down, faster and faster, while their little fly dapped the surface, first lightly here, then over there, all the while ever so gaily prancing and dancing and soon outdoing even *the* Dancing Fly itself.

"A little to your right," Timmy called, and Pinky moved a little to his right. I was dazedly rubbing my eyes with the back of my hand when I heard a watery explosion and then Pinky laughing and hollering, "Cleaned out our last pattern, Timmy, so I guess you gotta tie some more."

"Near quittin' time anyway," Timmy called back. "Better we get movin' before our pigeon does."

"Pigeon has already moved!" I hollered, popping out from behind my balsam and standing with proudly folded arms. "And thanks awfully, fellas, for reminding me there's more than one way to skin a cat."

Pinky wheeled and waved at me and sedately tipped his hat. "Hi!" he hollered. "You been eavesdripping up there very long?"

"Frenchman's biggest pigeon has seen all and heard all!" I cupped my hands and bawled like a train announcer in an empty station, my words echoing and echoing . . .

When finally they joined me up on the ridge and I'd resignedly paid off Pinky his double bet—it being, as I'd guessed, *his* turn to win—I cleared my throat and managed to inquire without my voice cracking just what magic fly had turned the trick.

"Your little Adams, of course," Timmy said.

"*My* little Adams?" I repeated dully, momentarily forgetting.

"Sure, sure, the very same fly you so generously told us about weeks ago but we so foolishly wouldn't believe you until approaching insolvency and desperation drove us to it." He wagged his head. "Trout simply go nuts over it, especially when it goes into its polka."

"Tell me," I murmured when I was able to go on, "how in the world did you ever dream up your astonishing joined-leader dropper-fly ploy? Or did you run across it somewhere?"

"Hell no," Timmy said. "One day I simply remembered Pinky's joshing remark last year about dapping flies from a balloon."

"I don't see the connection."

"Well, I figured ballooning really *was* one way to suspend a fly and also make it dance, however awkward." Timmy spread his hands. "Then I got to thinkin' about other possibly simpler ways to do the same thing—an' it took no great burst of Yankee ingenuity to come up with what you just seen."

"You're way too modest, Timmy," I said fervently. "I've been fishing ever since I shed diapers, and never have I seen or read or so much as heard of such a fantastic thing in all the ancient lore of angling. Why, it could revolutionize fishing—either that or ruin it." I wagged my head. "You—you ought to be in Congress, man."

"Don't get nasty."

191

"One more thing," I persisted weakly. "How do you guys ever get the damn leaders joined in the first place, fishing from opposite sides? Sounds like a real big deal."

"Easy, man," Timmy said. "When we start fishing, one of us casts a big bushy dry fly out maybe thirty–forty feet, somewhat at an angle, then the opposite guy pastes out a weighted nymph *over* the first cast, and then we both tighten and — bingo — the flies naturally hook and one of us simply reels in."

"But then you gotta tie on a dropper and all that," I persisted, morbidly determined to learn just how far I had been taken.

"No," Timmy said. "One of us keeps a permanent dropper on his leader, tied up about a foot or so. So all the reeler-in has to do is remove the old flies, join the two leaders, clap on a li'l ol' Adams—an' we're all set." He sighed. "Actually it's kinda like shootin' fish in a rain barrel, an' Pinky an' I been talkin' lately about goin' it alone."

"I've not only been taken but took," I said as I stared at the little man and wagged my head. "Indeed, there *is* more than one way to skin a cat," I dully repeated, screwing my rod case shut and hoisting my pack with a sigh.

"You're dead right there, pard," Timmy agreed, giving me a quirky smile and a wink, "just as maybe there's more'n one way to dance a fly."

"So I see," I said, for I saw.

16 *The Fishing Story Life Missed*

After writing three books, the cheering throngs of readers of which I could have accommodated nicely in a two-car garage—no, better make that one—I wrote my first novel, and all hell broke loose. While I still wonder what *that* book had that the others didn't, the fact is that my *Anatomy of a Murder* almost overnight got itself glued to the best-seller list, tapped by Book-of-the-Month, knighted by Otto Preminger (whose subsequent movie was graced by the presence of that gentle man Joseph N. Welch, who became a dear friend) and, as the royalties rolled in, blessed by the Internal Revenue Service.

Now the only reason I'm mentioning this is not to brag, heaven knows, but because the following story would be rather pointless if I didn't, since this background was the basis for there being any story to tell. For the painful truth is that, for all its material rewards, there is much about the trauma of bestsellerdom that is eminently forgettable. In fact if it weren't that my own immersion in it freed me to fish, for which I am eternally grateful, and

allowed me to get to know some talented and lovely people I would otherwise have missed, I doubt I would ever again mention it, even to myself.

Anyway, as my orbiting book and I joined hands and soared through the blazing hoops of national notoriety, I was naturally invited to appear and brandish my book on all manner of shows—talk shows, quiz shows, panel shows, possibly even dog shows—though here the memory bobbles a bit. Most of these bids I managed to turn down, especially after I discovered that a fisherman was more likely to raise a dead cat than a trout on the pastoral East River. But I did accept a few, and one of the most pleasantly memorable of these was when *Life* photographer Bob Kelley phoned me one day and asked if he might come up and follow me around fishing a few days, thus furnishing me with this story and starting a lasting friendship.

"You a fisherman, Mr. Kelley?" I parried cautiously.

"Yup," he said. "And I sure liked your book."

This was by now a familiar gambit that accompanied most of these invitations, and I tried not to wince. "Tell me, Mr. Kelley," I said, ever the tease, "and how did you like the movie?"

"Oh, that. I don't mean your courtroom yarn, though it wasn't too bad," Kelley said. "I mean your fishing book, *Trout Madness,* which I really liked. Main reason I called, in fact."

"Well, well," I said, beginning to purr.

"*Life* wants you to write the story to go with my pictures, for which they'll naturally pay," he ran on, naming a figure so generous it stunned me into silence. "Hello? Hello?" he shouted, clicking the phone. "You still on?"

194

"Barely, but rallying," I managed to say, already putty in the man's hands. "When would you plan to come up?"

"Midafternoon plane tomorrow," Kelley said. "How about it?"

"Fine, fine," I said before he could change his mind. "I'll meet your plane tomorrow."

So the next afternoon I met Bob Kelley's plane, then smiling, crew-cut, trench-coated Bob himself, who in turn presented me to a curly-headed towering young New Englander called Robert Brigham. "Moose is the reporter assigned to this one," Kelley explained as I pumped Moose's big paw.

"But I thought your magazine wanted me to write the story," I said, a little shaken.

"It still does," Bob Kelley said, shrugging and widening his hands. "But when our boss assigns a reporter to a case"—Bob rolled up his eyes and snapped his fingers—"*that* reporter tags along."

"Maybe Moose was sent to translate my stuff into English," I said, a little thoughtfully.

"Barely possible," Moose admitted in his Down East drawl. "That remains to be seen."

"Well, well," I said, rubbing my chin. "I'll try not to overwork you, Mr. Moose."

Clanking with cameras, luggage, and assorted equipment, the two Bobs and I repaired to the Mather Inn in my town and then for refreshments down in the bar, where Bob Kelley proceeded to outline his general plan. This, he explained, was for us somehow to try and show in words and pictures just what magical lure there was about trout fishing that would make a presumably intelligent man, one endowed with a four-karat legal educa-

195

tion, quit a more or less permanent job on his state's highest court and flee home to chase trout and write yarns about it. "What did make you do it?" Bob concluded.

"Just lucky, I guess," I said, "as the whore lady told the social worker when asked how *she* got that way."

"But seriously," Bob pleaded.

"That, Robert," I said, "is something I've been trying to explain to myself ever since—not to mention to my wife." I sighed. "But I'm willing to give it another try."

For the next three days Bob Kelley and I gave it the old college try, accompanied by our reporter, Bob Brigham, who had nothing to report, and whom we accordingly pressed into service as a combined rod bearer, camera toter, and ambulant bar. How did we make out? As my old fishing pal Luigi might have put it, "Lat me try an' tole you, my fran."

Part of the charm of trout fishing is that trout, unlike people, will respond only to quietude, humility, and endless patience, and as far as I was concerned Bob Kelley's trip richly confirmed that fact. It also proved some things trout will *not* respond to, one of them certainly being any fisherman who tries to show off and glorify himself at their expense. This sort of thing they seem to sense almost instantly by some mysterious telepathy running up through the rod and down the line and leader to the fly. Once this message is flashed, the trout seem to conspire to bring the poor wayward fisherman back to humility; either that or to the brink of nervous breakdown.

196

There was one other lesson all of us learned: that my Upper Peninsula of Michigan trout, at least, wanted no part in appearing on any photographic command performances ordered by anyone called Henry R. Luce. *That* message came through loud and clear.

Those first three days of fishing were a disaster as far as fishing pictures were concerned, and though I took the boys to some of the hottest spots I knew, I did not catch a single really decent trout. It seemed that I was so eager to provide Bob with a thrilling picture that I spent most of my time posing and posturing, either overstriking the few decent trout that did rise or, in my preoccupation with being photogenic, striking too late.

On the evening of the second day I did get on to one decent fighting brown when fate had poor Bob reloading his camera. By the time he'd shed that one and grabbed and focused another—he bristled with them—the bored brown had wound itself around an underwater snag and, as we heard my leader go *ping,* was merrily off and away.

In retrospect, as I write this it sweeps over me that this sort of thing has happened so often, not only then but since, that I'm prepared to swear that a fisherman is only at his relaxed best when he knows that nothing is watching him except the scampering chipmunks and God.

Bob was most understanding and nice about the whole thing, being a fisherman himself, but by the end of the third day the strain began to tell and even I could sense —in fact *that* was a good part of my trouble—that *Life* fully expected Bob to come up with at least one thrilling picture of a trophy trout being caught by that best-selling fly-casting author of *Trout Madness* because, after all, *Life* dealt in *success*.

197

When on the evening of the third day we finally gave

up we found Moose awaiting us back at the jeep deep in a novel, to which he'd sensibly turned on the morning of the second day when he saw how sad the fishing was.

"Any luck?" he dutifully inquired, pointing at the clinking drinks awaiting us on the hood of the car.

I widened my eyes and shrugged and raised my outstretched arms in the international sign language of defeat, and reached for my drink. "*Ah . . .* "

"Where to tomorrow?" Bob inquired glumly, still shedding cameras. "It better be good, for tomorrow's our last day."

"Really don't know yet," I said, "but I'll brood over it during the night. Meanwhile, if you will, Moosie boy, please pass the bourbon."

During the night inspiration struck—why hadn't I thought of it before?—and early the next morning we parked the jeep on the south side of the top of a deep valley through which ran one of the most sporting and wadable stretches of the entire Big Dead River. Though I rarely fished the place any longer because of my growing infatuation with brook trout, I had long known it harbored some of the biggest browns around.

"We rig up here, Bob," I said, leaping out and grabbing my waders and fighting my way into them as Bob did likewise while Moose yawned and settled down with his book.

"Moose," I said, when Bob and I were just about armed and ready for the last day's fray, "it's going to be a long day. Bob and I have a lot of river to cover. Wouldn't you like to tag along?"

"I'd sure like to," Moose eagerly said, "but I don't have any waders."

"No problem," I said. "I've got an old emergency pair way too big. Wear them."

My inspirations were coming in clusters and as Moose writhed his way into my old patched waders I had another. "Hell, Moose," I said, "there's a nice big pool where our trail hits the river. Why don't you take one of my extra rods and try for a trout while we do our stuff?"

"But I never fly-fished in my life," Moose confessed.

"Incredible. I thought all New Englanders were born holding a fly rod."

"Not this one. Only a little surf casting as a kid. Never held a fly rod in my hand."

"Then why did you and Kelley bother to buy fishing licenses?"

"Routine magazine policy to appease the local gendarmes. But I still can't cast a fly."

"Tell me, can you lace your shoes?" I asked.

"Of course."

"Then you can cast a fly," I said airily. "I'll rig you up a fiber glass nymphing rod you could heave a polecat with along with a stout leader and some big flies. All you got to do is keep pelting away. What do you say?"

"I'm game," Moose said, shrugging. "Beats reading bad novels."

So I rigged up Moose and handed him a tin box of faded and tattered old bucktail streamers and the three of us slid and slipped our way down the steep river trail to the first pool.

The omens were good. While no trout were rising in Moose's shaded pool, we soon spotted several spunky risers working between us and the first bend below.

"Let's go, master angler," Kelley said, champing at the bit.

"Bitterness will get you nowhere, Kelley," I said. "But first I got to give Moose a quick lesson." So saying, I towed Moose out into the current to give him casting room and, taking his rod, gave him a short cram course in casting a fly without impaling one's ear. "Now you try it," I said, handing him a rod, and Moose grabbed it and lashed out—and narrowly missed impaling *my* ear.

"Wait till we get out of here," I shrilled, scrambling, and Bob and I quickly splashed across to safety above his pool. "If time palls there's beer in the car icebox and you know where we hid the key," I called out to him above the sound of the current.

Moose nodded grimly and lashed out again, caught a dead branch behind him, jerked on it mightily and broke the branch, lost his balance and, amidst the crashing of falling timber, fell on his face in the river. "C- c- cold!" he sputtered, floundering to his feet and again falling, threshing and blowing like a beached whale. Bob and I averted our eyes and—it seemed the only decent thing to do—silently slipped away downstream on a worn fisherman's trail.

I shall mercifully spare any detailed account of the next four hours. It is enough to say that I fished over dozens and scores of rising browns, by far the best fish we'd seen on the trip; in fact, some of them real lunkers. But it was the same old story: in my zeal to please and play the role of master angler I kept striking too soon, too

late, too hard, too soft, too something . . . Box score: no trout. After about two frustating miles of this I looked sheepishly at Kelley and Kelley looked at his watch and shook his head.

"Too early for cocktails, Robert?" I inquired softly.

"I'd say just about four hours too late," Kelley said. "Let's get the hell out of here."

We took the shore trail upstream, resolutely ignoring all the lovely rises we saw along the way, and presently emerged on a high shaded bank overlooking Moose's pool.

"*Look!*" Kelley tensely whispered, pointing, and there in the middle of the pool, far over his flooded waders, stood an intent Moose fast to a simply massive rod-bending trout. Oblivious to our presence, Moose worked the threshing creature in, lunged at him with the net, missed, and as we watched, the big brown made a mighty flop and threw the fly and dashed away.

"Oh my Gawd," Kelley moaned in anguish, bowing his head.

Moose heard Kelley's lament and looked up and waved. "Hi, fellas," he called out cheerily. "How's the ol' luck?"

"Lousy," I said, "How about you?"

Moose turned his head and pointed inshore. "Got five dandy browns dressed out there in the ferns on account of no creel. Caught 'em the first coupla hours."

"*What!*" Kelley gasped.

"Lost three or four before I got the hang of the thing, one far bigger'n the slob that just got off."

"*What!*" I gasped.

"Lost track of how many I've caught and put back. Great fun, this fly-fishing." With that he slapped his big

202

fly down on the water with a tidal splash, there was a
savage roll and take, and Moose reared back like a bee-
stung shot-putter—and naturally snapped his leader
and lost his fly on another lunking trout. "That's it,"
Moose said, splashing his way ashore, dripping like a
tired water spaniel. "There goes my last fly."

"*My* last fly, you mean," I pensively corrected him.

"Let's go get a drink," Kelley said in an awed voice. "I
need the therapy."

Hours later, back around my kitchen table, I had my
final inspiration. "I've *got* it!" I said, slapping my leg.

"What's that?" Kelley said. "That we go make a midnight raid on the local fish hatchery?"

"The idea for your real fishing story," I ran on, all
aglow with my vision. "Look, fellas, it's simply perfect.
Here's this master fisherman you came a million miles to
photograph, the wily angler, the old fox, the guy who
writes books about his art—who after four days of
flailing falls flat on his—"

"Yes?" Kelley inquired silkily.

"Keister," I said, glancing over at my ironing wife.

"Go on."

"And there's good ol' Moose, who never held a rod in
his life, who threshes around like a mired mastodon in
one solitary pool, heaving out harpoons and flailing away
for hours like a man beating a rug—and who makes the
old master look like a bum." I spread my hands. "That's
your *real* story, boys. It's beautiful. I love it. And God
knows it's fishing."

Moose wagged his head. "We'd be fired," he said.

"What do you mean fired?" I said, looking at Kelley for
support.

"Moose is right," Kelley said, "We came here to do a

203

success story about a best-selling author and expert fly fisherman. That is our mission."

"So-called expert," I amended.

"No matter. Anything that tarnishes that halo of success—or maybe haloes don't tarnish—or dims the glittering image of our star is bad and verboten. The magazine'd never stand for it and we could indeed lose our jobs."

"Yes, I guess I see," I said after a spell, shaking my head. "In fact I'm awfully afraid I do see what you mean. But someday, I warn you, I'm going to tell it the way it was. And I do hope it won't get you boys fired."

"I'll drink to that," Bob said, and all of us clinked glasses and were shortly off to bed.

So the next day the boys caught their plane and I began working on my dubious success story, the main thing I recall about it being, as I brooded and pondered, that I came up with a thing I suspect more nearly expresses why *I* fish, at least, than anything I've written before or since. It was called "Testament of a Fisherman," which, I'd almost forgotten till now, first appeared in *Life* before it came out in Kelley's and my subsequent book, *Anatomy of a Fisherman,* now out of print.

That was at least a dozen years ago. Since then *Life* has folded its tent, of course, and Bob and Moose have moved on to greener pastures. But as I look back on it and consider my small part in it I can't help wondering whether *Life* wasn't sealing its own death warrant even then by so endlessly spinning its gilded fairy tales of "success," instead of telling it as it was. At least in its heedless death flight after this elusive will-o'-the-wisp I know of one grand fishing story it surely missed.

17 A Creelful of Short Casts

THE REEL-IN FLY

I am constantly amazed why we fishermen don't hear more about the fabulous reel-in fly or ever see it advertised or rhapsodized over in the fishing catalogs and outdoor magazines. Especially mystifying I find this conspiracy of silence when one stops to think that sometimes it is by all odds the most deadly attractive fly of all the scores of patterns we carry.

And what is this mysterious reel-in fly? one may ask. Well, while the precise pattern *is* a little hard to pin down, I'll grant, the rest is dead easy. The reel-in fly is any cotton-pickin' fly you happen to have on—wet, dry, or nymph—that the trout are so resolutely scorning that you finally let out a profane yelp and are disgustedly reeling it in to forever banish the damn thing when —*wham!*—you get the best strike of the day.

Only once in a 'coon's age do you ever *catch* this fish, of course, for the whole key to the magic effectiveness of the reel-in fly is your consuming desire to get the damn thing off and fast, so naturally you are totally unprepared for the strike when it

comes, and either rear back in shocked leader-snapping surprise or else are so stunned you strike too late. Nor can the strategy be faked, for the moment cunning sets in all its magic seems to flee because then one invariably fails to reel in with the required impatience and grand abandon.

Described most simply then, the reel-in fly is any lousy fly you ever fish on those exasperating occasions when it suddenly sweeps over you that the damned thing is so monumentally ineffective that you can't get rid of it fast enough, and you are reeling in with just the right amount of mindless petulance when all hell breaks loose. Perhaps it's just as well for the future of fishing that the strategy of fishing the reel-in fly can't ever be taught.

ON TYING ONE'S OWN

For some obscure reason, possibly an early fall out of my crib reaching for a bottle, I've never been able to learn to tie a decent fly. For years I took comfort telling myself that a fisherman needn't necessarily tie his own flies in order to have a ball fishing, that my own tieless career is living proof of that, and that if tying one's own was all that important, then, to be consistent, the complete angler ought also to build his own rod, weave his own line, fashion his own waders and, to go the whole hog, dig the ore and then smelt and forge his own bloody hooks.

But all along I deceived myself, for the longer I fish the stronger I feel that the fly is by far the most important thing in that fragile web of illusion and deceit that the successful fisherman weaves when he lures one of nature's wiliest creatures into mistaking a bent pin adorned with assorted fluff for something good to eat. Compared with the lordly fly, I now see, all else among a fisherman's prolific gear is mere fancy window dressing.

So while I still loyally believe that a fisherman can have himself a ball fishing the flies of another (else I'd have quit long ago), I now further believe he might have an even bigger ball if he fished with his own. The situation is akin to the thrill a concert pianist must feel playing one of his own compositions rather than a stranger's. If in addition the happy tyer also built his own fly rod, say, *that* would be like Rachmaninoff playing and conducting from the keyboard his own Second Piano Concerto.

The nontying fisherman learns this lesson the hard way, of course, by enduring the repeated frustration of coming upon a spirited rise of trout feeding on a fly hatch he can't seem to match with any of the forests of flies he totes around and, equally frustrating, can't seem to describe or explain to his favorite tyer. Another teaser is finally to luck upon a fly that is driving them wild and then—*ping*—suddenly lose this unique treasure on an overstrike or snag or lurking bough and be helpless either to replace or describe it. Or when he—but why torture myself with further illustrations?

While there are those rare occasions, of course, when feeding trout will hit even a rusty shoehorn (indeed, I once caught a gorgeous trout on a fly *I* had tied, a comic tumbleweed creation), there are those other and more frequent occasions when the choosy rascals will scorn anything but the right fly fished just the right way.

One such memorable occasion was the afternoon Hank and I were fishing that big old beaver dam up on

207

Gagliardi Creek. Though lovely wild brook trout were
rolling all around us, nothing seemed to work, especially
pride-eroding since we were out trying to pick up a few
nice ones for a Last Day fish fry for our gang to be held
the very next day.

Hank and I kept poring over our fly boxes, changing
flies, making fruitless casts, again poring over our boxes
. . . Finally, Hank waded around a far bend seeking
fishier pastures while I kept up the ritual of poring,
changing, casting. Suddenly Hank let out a curdling
whoop and I cupped my ear to catch the word.

"Big Muddler!" I heard him calling from far away.
"Switch to a big Muddler Minnow! Swim it slow!"

So once again I raided my fly boxes and came up with a
battered old Muddler that splashed like a skidding mal-
lard when I hurled it away from me. When finally the
landing wake subsided I'd barely begun swimming it
back to me when a speckled darling gaffled it, I let out a
whoop, and presently netted and creeled a twelve-inch
beauty.

"*Yippee!*" I yelped, again casting my bread upon the
waters.

When Hank and I met around dusk we had both filled
out with lovely catches of wild brooks—all on the
unlikely old Muddler. Yet, I still suspect that if Hank
hadn't possessed either the inspiration or desperation to
try this old paintbrush, our Last Day supper would likely
have been troutless.

As a consequence of my early crib fall I've naturally
been buying and scrounging flies as long as I've been
flinging them. And that goes back a mighty long way,

back to when the present Abercrombie store in Chicago was called Von Lengerke and Antoine and a crew-cut fly-tying and fishing whiz called Paul Stroud presided over the fishing department, then still on the ground floor. (Hank and I have fished with Paul up here; hence I *know* he was a whiz.)

I suppose I could fill a small telephone book with the names of all the fly tyers I've known and made love to over the years, but I'll content myself (and spare others) by saluting just a few local craftsmen who have kept me in business for so many years, old friends like Bill Nault, "Long John" Peterson (and his father before him), and Lloyd Anderson and, more recently, younger tying hands like Jerry Wozniak and teen-aged John Swartout of Petoskey.

I have fished with all of these lovely fly tyers—when I wasn't bugging them to tie up this or that special creation —all lucky guys who tie their flies with such grace and artistry that I sometimes wistfully wish I hadn't tumbled from that crib and might at least occasionally manage to "play" one of my own cotton-pickin' "compositions."

OUR WADING SCIENTISTS

Endlessly I am fascinated by those earnest fishermen who go about their fishing as though they were tackling a problem in higher calculus, any chance of the solution of which depends solely upon cerebration and a metric slide rule. Every aspect of their fishing betrays their devotion to the iron discipline of <u>Science</u>, capitalized and underlined.

All their flies, for example, are neatly sorted and

squirreled away in labeled, compartmentalized boxes strictly according to size, type, and pattern. In fact, I knew one such perfectionist who bristled with so many boxes that he had finally to give each fly a number and whip out a master chart and then frisk himself to track one down—a sort of planned-chaos switch, one might call it, on the informal jungle disorder of most fishermen's flies.

And awesome are their preparations before ever going fishing. While I have always thought that the best time to go fishing is when you can get away, my scientific brethren scoff at any such simplistic crudity. *They* wouldn't dream of going on a fishing trip—wups, I mean mounting a fishing expedition—without first going through a complicated preparatory ritual that is little short of incantatory.

First there are the latest barometric pressures, humidity readings and wind directions to be consulted and calibrated, followed by studies of tidal impulses, moon phases and assorted lunar tables often supplemented by delvings into last-minute radar sweeps and chill factors, not to mention occasionally consulting, I sometimes suspect, soggy tea leaves, the latest pollen count, and even Ann Landers. All this sounds mighty fascinating and doubtless impresses the fish no end but is something I have so far resisted mainly because, after all that, there can't be a hell of a lot of time left over to catch a fish.

These calculating fishermen naturally know the calibrations of their leaders down to the finest hair, both fore and aft, and, speaking of hair, most of them carry yards and yards of tippet material spun so incredibly fine and fragile that one can't help suspecting it must have

211

been riskily pilfered from the heads of sleeping Scandinavian princesses.

They scorn calling any fish or fly by its common name, of course, and will openly wince when such uncultured characters as I ever uncouthly refer to a speckled trout as a brookie instead of *Salvelinus fontinalis.* No move is made without prolonged calculation, and once upon the water they often seem to spend half their time skimming off or netting naturals and the balance crouching over their portable tying kits trying to match before nightfall what it is they've found.

These tinkertoy fishermen have many other tricks up their sleeves, of course, but I'm afraid I lack both the patience and savvy even to list them since so many of their maneuvers I never could understand anyway. Moreover, since all of us fishermen are the very souls of tolerance, I have heard, I feel compelled in all fairness to add that I suppose they have as much right to fish and carry on their way as I have mine. I further suspect they couldn't change their way if they wanted, which after all only reflects their basic drives and is, if the truth were only known, probably also the way they make love.

All of which allows me to end with the happy thought that any skeptical gal wanting a sneak preview of what might lie in store, while still keeping her virtue intact, might better first accompany the boyfriend fishing before joining him in the sack. Then again, tastes do vary, and I read somewhere recently—possibly in a golf manual—that some ladies indeed respond to a lot of preliminary maneuverings, which the manual rather technically labeled, as I recall, something called foreplay —but then again (old fishermen grow so forgetful) might simply have been "Fore!"

FIRST DAY, LAST DAY

Fishing is essentially a lonely pursuit I have learned; best enjoyed in solitude, one's sense of isolation from the scurrying man-swarm being in itself a good part of the fun. And since I go fishing almost every day all summer long while most other fishermen have to work, I would naturally find myself fishing alone a lot anyway, whether I happened to like it that way or not.

Even when I'm accompanied in my fishing it's usually by but one other fisherman, only rarely by two, and even then we quickly separate when we get there, often never to see each other till it's time to quit. And yet this persistent aura of unsociability that attends fishing lies less in any ingrained aloofness of us fishermen, I suspect, than in the nature of the sport itself, and I'd like to offer some evidence to prove it.

A gang of us local fishermen gets together at least twice a year and sometimes oftener, solitude be damned. Our set dates are the first and the last days of fishing, with an occasional spontaneous get-together in between (maybe to escape traffic) on such holidays as July Fourth and Labor Day. Our only bond is that we are friends and fellow fishermen, and our ages are often as disparate as our trades, the latter currently ranging from bartenders to chemists. (I tried for an A to Z thing but couldn't quite make it, because, drat it, our lone zebra breeder has moved away.)

And what do we do? Well we fish, of course, but not too seriously, and like mostly to sit around an open fire and

compare and exchange flies and fishing fairy tales and
generally frolic and overfeed (and drink) and, when the
day is far spent, grope our way home. If one of us has
faltered and soared heavenward on creaking wings since
our last session, we'll raise a cup to his memory, less in a
spirit of melancholy, I swear, than in wistful regret that
he can't be there to enjoy the day.

Some of the fishermen at these sessions I fish with
regularly, others occasionally, and some but rarely during the regular season, if at all. And the gap in our ages, if
not quite nine to ninety, is sometimes marvelous to behold.

At one such recent conclave, for example, our
youngest fisherman was but nineteen and the oldest
eighty-nine (my old friend and cribbage partner, Gurn S.
Webb), followed by the late L. P. "Busky" Barrett, then in
his early eighties, with Hal Lawin and I running neck and
neck, closing in fast on our three-score-and-ten.

Then came the younger set, such as Don Anderson
crowding sixty and, one of my oldest living fishing pals,
"young" Hank Scarffe, reaching an incredible fifty, followed by such fumbling adolescents still in their thirties
and forties as Ted Bogdan, Anthony "Gigs" Gagliardi,
Mike Kelly, Harry Koenig, Joe Overturf, Lou Rosen-
baum, John "The Builder" Walbridge (he built my fishing shack and bridge), and Jerry Wozniak (notice how
slyly alphabetical the old fisherman is), our "baby" being
bearded Tom Bogdan in his teens.

How these droll sessions ever got started is lost in the
mists of memory. But I can recall, not without a pang,

215

that over the years I have moved from being one of the youngest to attend them on to being one of the very oldest, a wry circumstance I choose to ignore (perhaps itself a sign of galloping senility) just as long as I can still look forward to celebrating the First and Last Day along with my fellow fishermen.